MURDER AT MARLHILL

Was Harry Gleeson innocent?

BY
Marcus Bourke

Published in Ireland by
Geography Publications,
Kennington Road,
Templeogue, Dublin 6W.

Copyright © 1993 Marcus Bourke

ISBN 0 906602 23 8

Cover design by Christy Nolan, from photographs of Harry Gleeson and Mary McCarthy's house.
Typesetting by Phototype-Set, Glasnevin, Dublin 9.
Printed by Colour Books, Baldoyle Industrial Estate, Dublin 13.

THIS BOOK IS DEDICATED TO MARY GLEASON OF
COLUMBIA, SOUTH CAROLINA, HARRY GLEESON'S LAST
SURVIVING SIBLING, NOW IN HER 105th YEAR AND AS
FIRM A BELIEVER IN HER BROTHER'S INNOCENCE AS
EVER.

Introduction

It was in 1988 that I first encountered the Gleeson case. Somewhere in the triangle of the Golden Vale bounded by Cashel, Golden and Cahir I overheard a conversation about a murder that had occurred near New Inn during World War II. Both speakers insisted that the man hanged for the crime had not committed it. One also said that the distinguished lawyer Seán MacBride, who had defended Gleeson, still believed almost 50 years later that his client was innocent.

Interviewed in 1974, 33 years after Gleeson's execution, MacBride said: "I was quite convinced that . . . Gleeson not alone didn't commit the crime, but couldn't have committed it as . . . he was elsewhere at the time". Two years earlier in 1972 MacBride had said: "I was quite certain the man was innocent. I had no doubt about it . . . I did everything I could to prevent him from being executed".

The more I learned about the Gleeson case the more impressed I became by Sean MacBride's lifelong view of the wrongness of the jury's verdict. I was particularly struck by the fact that the late John Dalton of Cloughaleigh near Golden, a prominent figure who knew Gleeson, never wavered in his belief in Gleeson's innocence. Moreover, to me the conspiracy of silence which surrounded the case – and which I suspect still partly surrounds it – seemed to reveal an aspect of Irish rural society of the time which merited exposure.

For advice, co-operation and assistance in the research that has gone into this book I am indebted to many people. Without access to the MacBride Papers and to the file of the late John J. Timoney, solicitor, I could not have even begun this research. Accordingly, to Ms. Caitriona Lawlor of Dublin, custodian of the MacBride Papers, and to Mr. Brendan Jones, solicitor, of Tipperary, I am grateful for this access. To Mrs. Anna White (formerly MacBride) and Ms. Louie O'Brien, both of Dublin, I am also grateful. I acknowledge the co-operation of the staffs of the National Archives, the National Library of Ireland, the Co. Library in Thurles and the *Nationalist* newspaper in Clonmel. To Ms. Helen Meaney of the *Irish Times* and Ms. Fiona Daly, solicitor, and to others (both in Dublin and Tipperary) who read drafts of some or all of the chapters, I am thankful for their criticism and advice.

To Annelies Coghlan my thanks go for typing the manuscript; similarly to Stephen Hannon for preparing the maps. For designing the cover I am indebted to Christy Nolan, and for his usual skill in typesetting my thanks go to Michael Lynam of Phototype-Set. Colour Books produced the type of professional printing that is now expected of them.

At local level in Co. Tipperary I could not have managed without the advice and encouragement of Eddie Dalton of Golden and Paddy Leamy of Marlhill, the latter a brother-in-law of one of the Guards in New Inn in 1941. The benevolent influence of the late Fr. James Meehan, then parish priest of New Inn, solved some awkward problems. To Sergt. Duffy of the Garda Museum, to Garda officers in Co. Tipperary and to officials in the Dept. of Justice in Dublin, who tried unsuccessfully to trace documents mysteriously missing – in particular, the District Court depositions – I am also grateful. The practical help volunteered by people in the New Inn area, who participated in technical experiments, is acknowledged. So is the photographic expertise of Jim Connolly and Brendan Burke, both of Dublin.

Marcus Bourke,
October 1993.

Sources

There were four principal sources for this book – (i) the National Archives files of the Central Criminal Court and the Court of Criminal Appeal; (ii) the Seán MacBride Papers; (iii) the client file on the Gleeson case of the late John J. Timoney, solicitor, Tipperary; and (iv) the contemporary newspapers of Clonmel, Thurles and Dublin. Seán MacBride mentioned the case in two published interviews – in *The Word* magazine (December 1972) and in the *Sunday Independent* (8 December, 1974). The late Una Troy (daughter of Judge Troy) used the McCarthy family in her novel *We Are Seven* (London, 1955).

In addition, information was received from Knockgraffon school roll, New Inn parish register, the firearms register kept in Feehan's store, Cashel and the Garda Museum, Dublin. A number of local people in the New Inn area supplied information, either from their own memories of the case or from what they had been told by an older generation now dead. Relatives of Harry Gleeson also supplied useful information.

In Sergt. Daly's native county both oral and written information regarding this officer was received from local sources. Finally, information, advice and interpretation were received regarding technical matters such as ballistics (including tests carried out in the New Inn area), and official weather reports were used for the period of the murder in 1940.

Marcus Bourke has family connections with Tipperary. He is a barrister and served in the Attorney-General's office as a legislative draftsman for over twenty-five years. He has written biographies of the Fenian leader John O'Leary (1967), the 1916 republican The O'Rahilly (1967) and G.A.A. founder, Michael Cusack (1989). The second edition of his *History of the G.A.A.*, first published in 1980, came out in 1990. He is editor of the *Tipperary Historical Journal*.

Contents

		Page
Introduction		00
Sources		
Chapter 1	'CLEAR MY NAME'	1-10
Chapter 2	'MOLL'S FOXY HEAD'	11-22
Chapter 3	A CASE TO ANSWER	23-36
Chapter 4	'A CRAFTY, COLD-BLOODED MURDER'	37-52
Chapter 5	GLEESON'S DEFENCE	53-64
Chapter 6	HARRY IS HANGED	65-76
Chapter 7	A FAIR TRIAL?	77-86
Chapter 8	CONSPIRACY OF SILENCE	87-102
Chapter 9	TOMMY REID GIVES HARRY GLEESON AN ALIBI	103-107
Appendix I	Exhibit 10	108-122
Appendix II	*Dramatis Personae*	123

Chapter 1

'Clear my name'

At eight o'clock on the morning of Wednesday 23 April, 1941 Harry Gleeson was hanged in Mountjoy Jail in Dublin for the murder of his neighbour Mary McCarthy. Her body had been found in a remote spot on Gleeson's uncle's farm near New Inn in Co. Tipperary early on Thursday 21 November, 1940. Nine days later, on 30 November, Gleeson was arrested and charged with the murder. A six-day preliminary hearing in Clonmel District Court in January 1941 was followed by a ten-day jury trial in Green Street courthouse in Dublin in February. A four-day hearing in the Court of Criminal Appeal a month later and a reprieve campaign both failed, and the posting outside the jail gates of the customary notice by a prison official at 8.05 a.m on the morning of 23 April recorded the execution of Gleeson.

Gleeson was attended by two chaplains from nearby Clonliffe College just before he mounted the scaffold at 7.55 a.m. The previous night he had been visited by a Capuchin friar, Fr. Ferdinand, OFM Cap. As required by law, the execution was witnessed by the prison governor, the prison doctor and the local sheriff. In accordance with customary practice the Government had brought over the official British hangman, Albert Pierrepoint, who died as recently as 1992, many years after he had become an opponent of capital punishment. Of Pierrepoint it was said that, to steady his nerves, he smoked a cigar on the platform, pausing between two puffs to pull the lever that opened the trap-door on which stood the convicted man, hooded and bound. After the body was taken down a brief formal inquest was held, and the body was then interred inside the prison grounds. Meanwhile, outside the prison gates the usual small group of morbid "spectators" dispersed quietly after they had read the notice posted up just after the hanging.

That afternoon, in his home in Clonskea on the south side of Dublin, the brief report in the evening newspapers of the hanging was read with more than usual interest by Sean MacBride. He had defended Gleeson in all three courts and personally organised the campaign for Gleeson's reprieve. Although still only in his mid-thirties, MacBride had already had a colourful career. The son of the executed 1916 leader, Major John MacBride, he had been brought up in Paris when his parents went their different ways. While in his teens he took part in the War of Independence, and was a junior member of the Irish delegation which travelled to London in 1921 to negotiate the Anglo-Irish Treaty. Strongly opposed to the Treaty, he went underground, becoming Chief of Staff of the post-1922 IRA. In 1936 he broke with the military wing of extreme republicanism and became a journalist. In 1937 he was called to the Bar, where he soon built up a big criminal practice. Ahead of him still lay an outstanding public career – Senior Counsel before he was forty, Minister for External Affairs (as leader of the new party, Clann na Poblachta) from 1948 to 1951, international figure campaigning for basic human rights, and winner of both the Nobel and Lenin Peace awards before his death in 1988.

From the day early in December 1940 when he took on Gleeson's case, Sean MacBride was convinced of his client's innocence, a view he held to the day he died almost forty-six years later. By coincidence he knew that part of Co. Tipperary where the murder was committed, having friends in Cahir (the nearest town to New Inn) from whom he got the inside story of the crime. It was, he told close friends as recently as 1985, the miscarriage of justice in the Gleeson case that motivated him to press for the abolition of capital punishment, not achieved until twenty-three years after Gleeson's execution. Within days of being retained by Gleeson's solicitor, John J. Timoney, MacBride visited New Inn and, with Timoney and Gleeson's relatives, inspected the scene of the murder, meticulously noting every detail of the landscape and returning shortly afterwards for a second visit. Much more than with the other two lawyers who acted for him, Gleeson in the last four months of his life built a special rapport with Sean MacBride. The day before he was hanged – Tuesday 22 April – Gleeson asked for a last visit from Sean MacBride. That evening the lawyer and future Minister arrived at Mountjoy jail for an experience he remembered for the rest of his life. In a letter he wrote to Timoney from notes he took down in his car outside the jail, MacBride described this last poignant meeting with his doomed client.

"He asked me to let his uncle and aunt and his friends know that he did not mind at all dying, as he was well prepared, and that he would pray for them as soon as he reached Heaven. He was quite calm and happy. He assured me several times that he would not like to change places with anyone else, as he felt sure that he had undergone his purgatory in this world and that he might never have such an opportunity of being so well prepared to meet his death. He was quite cheerful and chatted freely about his execution. He asked me to specially thank you for all the work you had done on his behalf, and said he would pray for you."

"At the end of the interview he stood up and said: 'The last thing I want to say is that I will pray tomorrow that whoever did it will be discovered, and that the whole thing will be like an open book. I rely on you then to clear my name. I have no confession to make, only that I didn't do it. That is all. I will pray for you and be with you if I can, whenever you, Mr. Nolan-Whelan and Mr. Timoney are fighting and battling for justice'." MacBride continued: "I took a note of these words afterwards. He uttered these words with feeling and a certain amount of emotion. As you know, he was not usually very fluent or eloquent in speaking. He was on this occasion. That was the last I saw of Henry Gleeson. I understand he remained quite calm and happy right to the end." Thirty-three years later Sean MacBride said he had been "shattered" by this meeting.

Harry Gleeson was born in 1903 near Holycross, some twenty miles north of New Inn. One of twelve children of Thomas Gleeson and Catherine Caesar, he grew up on a prosperous farm. Educated at the local national school at Gaile, Harry by his late teens was an athletic youth, almost six feet tall. A good hurler, he played well into his late twenties with Rockwell Rovers after he moved to New Inn. Coming from a musical family, Harry could play the fiddle from an early age, and became an exceptionally gifted fiddler after he perfected his technique under a traditional teacher named Dick Cantwell in Cashel, who taught him to read a score. Harry also developed a lifelong passion for breeding greyhounds, and to the day of his arrest spent much of his spare time training dogs. Around 1920 Gleeson, who had been reared by a maternal uncle, was offered employment by another uncle, John Caesar, who then farmed near New Inn. Caesar, also from Holycross, had won an All-Ireland hurling medal with Tipperary in 1899, and spent some years in his youth in the United States, where amongst other jobs he had worked on the building of the famous Brooklyn Bridge in New York. In 1917 he returned with his modest savings to Tipperary, where he "married into" a farm near New Inn. In 1928 when his first wife died he sold the farm, remarried and moved a mile or so to a 75-acre farm at Marlhill. By the late 1930s, when almost seventy, he had left the management and the working of the farm to his nephew. Since the Caesars were childless, Harry Gleeson would in due course probably inherit the place.

From the day he arrived in New Inn Harry Gleeson was well liked locally. Open, friendly, with an extrovert personality, he mixed easily with the New Inn community, frequently playing his fiddle at informal functions in their homes. Although he never developed a lasting friendship with a woman, he was sought after as a dancing partner, and at least one woman still alive in New Inn remembers dancing with him at a function in the local coursing club only three days before his arrest on 30 November 1940. With a friend from the Rossmore area, also still alive, Harry formed a partnership which carried out harvesting operations all over south County Tipperary in the Autumn of 1940. By his uncle, his neighbours and other good judges of farming in the area he was widely recognised as an efficient, industrious, even meticulous, farm manager. Devoted to the uncle and aunt with whom he had lived for over twenty years, without any apparent enemies in the parish, well thought of by the local clergy and on excellent terms with the Caesars' other employee Tommy Reid, Harry would have made an ideal partner for a local girl.

Also living in with the Caesars was another relative of theirs, Tommy Reid, then in his early twenties, who by 1940 had been working for Caesar for nine years. A quiet hard-working youth, he had come to look on Mrs. Caesar as his mother, and was to display remarkable loyalty to Gleeson – with consequences he could not anticipate. Probably because of the age-gap between him and Harry, Reid had his own circle of local friends, with whom he usually spent his evenings. The dominant figure in the Caesar household was Mrs. Caesar, whose maiden name was Hogan and who was from West Tipperary. With a strong personality, she made all the domestic decisions. A deeply religious woman , she was on friendly terms with the local parish priest, Fr. James O'Malley, a regular visitor to the house and a frequent recipient of donations from Mrs. Caesar. The fact that the entire household came from outside the New Inn area, while tending to unite them as a family unit, was to have serious consequences after the murder, when local reluctance to co-operate with the Guards manifested itself.

Amongst the Big Houses dotted round the countryside near New Inn in 1940, one is of particular importance in this book – Garranlea House, then the home of the Cooneys, a wealthy Catholic landowning family, who had once owned several hundred acres of rich farming land, until in the 1920s it was acquired by the State and sub-divided. The family, however, still remained both prosperous and influential. One of them, Anastasia (Anna), who had been a nurse during World War I, was prominent in local charitable work. In 1940 she was president of the local guild of the Catholic lay body, the Legion of Mary. Her work in the Legion put her on close terms with the parish priest. Indeed, events in New Inn both before and after the murder suggested that Miss Cooney acted as the eyes and ears of Fr. O'Malley, who relied on her local knowledge of many of his parishioners, especially the poorer people, with whom he would normally have little contact.

Lying on the main Dublin to Cork road halfway between the towns of Cashel and Cahir, New Inn was then (as it still is today) a typical, pleasant, undistinguished cross-roads village. With only a handful of private houses, it consisted of two shops, three pubs, two schools, a petrol-station, a convent, two cemeteries and a police station manned by a sergeant and three Guards. In June 1940 a new Sergeant, Anthony Daly, arrived, and three months later a new Superintendent, Patrick Mahony, took up duties in the nearby town of Cahir. Situated in the heart of the rich farming area known as the Golden Vale, New Inn had a hinterland of prosperous farms and even bigger horse-racing stables. In this respect Tipperary has changed little in fifty years, horses, hounds and hurling still lying heavily on peoples' minds!

Life in rural Tipperary in the late 1930s for the average medium-sized farmer like John Caesar was comfortable, if simple and basic. At a time when official hand-outs were almost unknown, prosperity was relative and demanded careful husbandry, prudent financial management and even occasional privation. No doubt Tipperary was luckier than other counties because of the spirit of self-reliance being fostered by the new rural body, Muintir na Tire. However, in September 1939, little more than a year before the murder of Mary McCarthy, the German invasion of Poland signalled the start of World War II, a conflict in which this country decided to remain neutral. Neutrality, however, called for sacrifices by all; so a state of emergency was declared by the Government. Amongst the measures adopted early in 1940 in order to ensure supplies of basic food was compulsory tillage. To guard against a possible invasion by either warring group, a national auxiliary military body was set up, the Local Security Force, predecessor of the present F.C.A. By mid-1940 the L.S.F. numbered 200,000. Among the 8,000 members in Co. Tipperary was the veteran IRA leader Jack Nagle, who became leader of the New Inn A group. Second in command of the New Inn B group, whose duty it was to augment the Guards, was one Thomas Hennessy, soon to be pushed into prominence by the McCarthy murder case.

To an extent that is difficult to appreciate today, the Catholic Church in 1940 had an enormous influence on the daily life of the community. As Tim Pat Coogan once put it, it "shaped the thought-moulds of 95 per cent of the nation", a state of affairs that was to continue for another thirty years. As this book will show, when a major crisis such the New Inn murder hit a local community it was to their parish priest that people went for guidance and leadership. At a higher level, the annual Lenten pastoral of each bishop became a kind of diocesan policy document, spilling over into politics and economic policy. In this respect the 1940 Lenten pastoral of Archbishop Kinane, in whose diocese New Inn lay, was no exception. The towns of Tipperary, he stated, were already affected by the war; trade was down and unemployment up, and the cost of living rising, leading to greater poverty. Nevertheless, " to moderate the violence of our passions", the customary strict Lenten fast and abstinence regulations were again promulgated – only one main meal daily, no meat at any other meal, and no meat at all on Fridays.

Archbishop Kinane also used his pastoral to clarify the position of the Church on illegal organisations like the IRA, then flourishing in his diocese. Membership of such bodies was, he stated, sinful and forbidden to Catholics; the aim of the IRA, he claimed, was to establish a socialist republic. This portion of the pastoral was a reminder of how fresh memories of the Civil War still were in Tipperary, the southern half of which had been the principal scene of republican activities from 1922 to 1924. Moreover, all through the 1930s, as the archbishop knew, Tipperary had continued to provide recruits for the IRA. The area around New Inn was particularly active in this respect, and both the Guards and the IRA were obliged to rely heavily on information supplied by informers. This in turn led to a continuation of the traditional distrust of the police, a side-effect of which was the reluctance of many people in the New Inn area to co-operate with police enquiries into a case like the McCarthy murder.

It was one of the paradoxes of a society so dominated by Catholic culture as rural Tipperary that Mary McCarthy could exert so much influence on her community. Born in 1902 to an unmarried mother (also Mary McCarthy), Moll Carthy, as she was known locally, is believed to have been reared and educated at an orphanage in Clonmel. In her teens she obtained domestic employment from farmers in New Inn. Only five feet five inches in height and of attractive appearance, Moll had distinctive red hair. Between 1921, when only 19, and May 1940, when 38, she had seven children – Mary, Patrick, Michael, Ellen, Bridget, Cornelius and Margaret (Peggy). It is believed that she also had several still-born children. Six of the seven reputed fathers of the children born alive were local residents, the other being from outside Tipperary. The identities of all were known in New Inn, and to some extent still are today, as is the identity of her own reputed father, a local farmer. The seventh child, Peggy, born six months before Moll's murder, survived for only a few weeks. The identity of Peggy's father was never revealed by Moll, not even to her local intimates. Exhaustive enquiries made at the time, and again more recently, could only narrow his identity down to three or four local men and one living some miles from New Inn. There was even a local theory that Moll herself did not know. Moll Carthy lived frugally in the heart of this prosperous farming region. Her tiny home consisted of a primitive, dilapidated two-roomed, single-storied cottage by the roadside, with a thatched (later corrugated iron) roof. This "hovel", as a local newspaper called it in 1940, had also been that of her mother, and is marked on the 1904 Ordnance Survey map. The Carthy cottage was surrounded on three sides by the farm of John Caesar, Harry Gleeson's home and workplace for most of his adult life.

On a two-acre field adjacent to her cottage Moll kept a greyhound, a donkey, and a small herd of goats – two of these being "pucks", for whose stud services she charged a fee. A few, but only a few, neighbours, among them John Caesar and his wife, supplied some of the Carthys' basic foodstuffs and firewood. So did some of the lay staff of Rockwell College, the exclusive boarding school which had an extensive farm nearby. From the State Moll received the princely sum of six shillings (30p) a week in home assistance, and a weekly allowance of free milk – less than two pints a day for her household of six. Amongst those who supplied her with potatoes were the Caesars, Harry Gleeson and another neighbour, John Halpin and his wife. Clearly a survivor, Moll Carthy presided over a harmonious household, a fact once formally established to the satisfaction of the law. Her six children, each of whom attended the local national school at Knockgraffon, were devoted to their mother and she to them. When her eldest son secured employment at a local farm a mile from home, he usually visited his mother every evening. Locally it was understood that each child of Moll Carthy, as he or she grew up, was told of the identity of his or her father. It was also admitted locally that she never consorted with more than one man at a time. Each in turn declined to marry her (so the local story went), and in time abandoned her, to be succeeded by another. That these alliances were known publicly is beyond doubt. When I began to research this case fifty years after Moll's death, the identities of her various partners were still known in New Inn.

The existence of women like Moll Carthy in non-urban areas in the first half of this century has gone largely unnoticed by social and historical commentators. It is known that for much of the previous century, and until the withdrawal in 1922 of the British garrison, a serious social and health problem existed in some garrison towns. However, it would be naive to assume that this phenomenon was non-existent outside our towns, and there is no reason to think that Co. Tipperary was exceptional in this respect. Socially women like Moll Carthy were treated as outcasts; the attitudes of Fr. O'Malley and Miss Cooney, both of whom befriended Moll Carthy, were exceptional for the time.

In the tightly-knit community that was New Inn of the 1920s and 1930s, Moll Carthy's unconventional life-style did not pass unnoticed. Her activities, and her continued residence in the area, became a source of tension, especially among the immediate families and the close relatives of the men who had fathered her children. Since a father's identity was not immediately apparent, it became necessary to await the growth to childhood (or even later) of each child, before his or her physical features could be matched with those of one of several reputed fathers. After the birth of her first two children, opposition to Moll Carthy took a drastic form. In 1926, when her mother was living with her and before Caesar and Gleeson had come to Marlhill at all, her thatched roof was set on fire one night in an attempt to kill all four residents as they slept. That this was no accident is evident from the deliberate burning the same night of a vacant cottage nearby, lest the Carthys (if they escaped) should move into it. Because of the malicious nature of the two fires, Moll went to law, and was awarded £25 (a substantial sum then) for malicious damage to her roof. Soon after this, as a result of pressure by some parishioners according to local accounts, the parish priest of New Inn, Fr. Edward Murphy, condemned Moll from the altar. She was feared simply because she did not conform. She was then a regular churchgoer, but there is no local memory of the parish priest having condemned the arson attack on her home. In 1932 Fr. Murphy was succeeded by Fr. O'Malley, a more easy-going, even liberal-minded, man who had served for 12 years in New Zealand. He replaced his predecessor's policy by a more tactful approach to Moll. By the mid-1930s, however, as the number of Carthy children continued to increase, a case had been made for a return to the Murphy tactics. Since the men of New Inn were not prepared to exert pressure on Fr. O'Malley, some of their womenfolk banded together informally and persuaded the new pastor to receive a delegation. This was patiently listened to, but without any promise of what the women would regard as firm action against Moll.

Fr. O'Malley's indecision may have been influenced by the knowledge that his women parishioners were no more united than their men folk, for by now, as her brood grew, and as feeding and clothing them became increasingly difficult, Moll Carthy was befriended by Miss Cooney. The recent birth of a child whose father was known to be a married man had led to a break in Moll's friendship with Fr. O'Malley, but Miss Cooney took his place and doubtless kept him informed of developments. She even became the godmother of at least one Carthy child, and was the only woman ever known to have crossed Moll's threshold. Moves to curb Moll's activities came to a climax when the Guards applied to the District Court for the committal to State care of the Carthy children. The case came before District Justice Sean Troy, who showed himself to be even more tolerant than Fr. O'Malley. By skilful examination of the older children, he satisfied himself that the young Carthys were well fed and looked after, and dismissed the application. A similar application a couple of years later also failed.

As for Moll herself, her behaviour as she grew older suggested even more indifference to the social impact she must have known she was making on the community amongst whom she lived. It was as if her victory in the court and the hostility it revealed provoked her into flaunting her unorthodox way of life more openly. One day she arrived at the gate of Knockgraffon school as staff and pupils were leaving. She made a blistering verbal attack on all within earshot, the gist of which was that her children were as good as the rest and did not deserve to be shunned as if they were outcasts. At least one child was taken away from the school around this time. Meanwhile, she continued to bestow her favours. Although there must have been times when she and her family suffered real privation, there is also evidence that, in addition to assistance from charitable neighbours, she often received substantial quantities of unused or discarded food from Rockwell College. I have been informed that she even kept a record (a kind of visitors' book) of visitors, some of whom she later persuaded to return a favour, such as repairing her roof. Moreover, at least two police sergeants became regular visitors to her cottage. Also, for a time in the late 1930s she was employed, apparently on a temporary basis, doing domestic work in New Inn police station. In the files of Gleeson's solicitor is a contemporary record of a conversation with a local source which states that "the Guards used to have great gas with her" – this, inside the station, in the centre of the village.

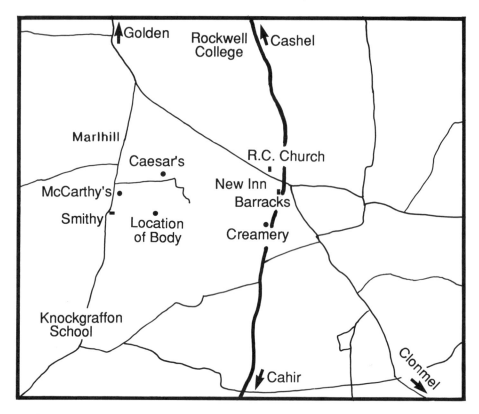

Marlhill and New Inn.

Chapter 2

'Moll's foxy head'

By 8.30 on the morning of Thursday 21 November, 1940 Harry Gleeson was going about his daily tasks on his uncle's farm in Marlhill. After the heavy rain of the previous night the day was dry but bitterly cold. Lighting a fire in the kitchen, and walking round in his stockinged feet lest he should disturb the elderly couple sleeping in a downstairs bedroom, he put on a kettle for the first round of tea of the day. Then climbing the stairs, boots in hand, he woke Tommy Reid. After the fire had been lit and breakfast was finished, the two men took a milk-pail to the "crib field", where each milked six cows, returning around 9.30 to the farmyard. There they left the full pails in the dairy for Mrs. Caesar. The pair then separated. Reid remained around the yard doing odd jobs. Gleeson put one of his three greyhounds on a lead to bring it for its morning exercise through the fields, a daily routine he had been following for many months, always taking the same route. As he went from field to field, Gleeson took the opportunity to count his uncle's sheep lest any were missing or had strayed. He also brought back a straying bull, which had wandered on to a neighbouring farm. As he got to the end of the third field, his hound now on the loose with no cattle in sight, Gleeson noticed that some bushes he had used some days earlier to block a gap into the next field had been pushed aside. He climbed partly up on the fence to see what had happened.

What he saw on the other side gave him a shock. A body, which from the clothes he knew to be a woman's, lay there apparently lifeless. On it sat a small black dog, which growled menacingly at Harry. Putting his hound back on the lead, Gleeson hurried home and told his uncle and aunt, still in bed, of his discovery. He then went at once for the Guards. Taking a short-cut through the fields by way of an old Mass path, he reached New Inn police station at 10.20 a.m. To Guard Vincent Scully, who met him inside the door of the station, Gleeson announced that he had come to report that he had found a woman's body on his uncle's land. He knew it was a woman, he explained, "by her petticoat [meaning her dress] and shoes". However, because an angry dog stood guard

11

nearby, he could not approach her to find out if she was dead or just asleep. Sergeant Daly, along with Guard Ruth, went at once with him by car back to Marlhill. Parking the car in Caesar's yard, the three men went through the land to the Dug-Out Field, so called from a man-made shelter dating back to the Civil War some 20 years before. As they approached the body they recognised it at once as that of Moll Carthy. Lying on her back near the boundary fence, she had been badly injured around the face and head. The position of her little dog, partly on top of the body, had concealed from Gleeson the full extent of the injuries.

Moll Carthy's death was naturally a sensation in the normally placid village of New Inn. She, her mother and her reputed father were all from the vicinity. Yet, to many people in New Inn her death must have been a cause for relief. Now that she was dead, the question naturally being asked locally was: who had done it, and why in such a brutal way? As a local newspaper reported, New Inn was "full of rumours". Between thirty and forty Guards were drafted in to search the fields; they even dragged drains and probed hedges. To local people the purpose of all this activity was a mystery, because it became known almost at once that Moll had been shot, one man even claiming to have heard the fatal shots. All the men in the locality who had known Moll were now probably checking or concocting alibis. If one includes the wives, adult children, parents and siblings of these men, there must have been dozens of people with a motive to kill her. A number of local men were in fact taken in for questioning but all were released, and several holders of firearms licences had their guns temporarily impounded for examination.

For the rest of Thursday 21 November, and until about midday on Friday 22 November, a permanent police guard was mounted on the body. At about 11.30 on Thursday morning a local priest administered the last rites. Around 1.30 p.m. Dr. James O'Connor from Cashel examined the body for the Guards; his findings were to prove of major significance. Then in mid-afternoon Superintendent Patrick Mahony of Cahir, the senior police officer for the area, arrived with a large waterproof lorry-cover, which he spread over the whole area where the body lay.

On Friday 22 November, at about 10.15 a.m., the State Pathologist, Dr. John McGrath, arrived in New Inn from Dublin. At Caesar's farm he made a preliminary examination of the body, still lying where it had been found twenty-seven hours earlier. He then ordered its removal to the police station. There, with Dr. O'Connor, he spent some hours conducting a detailed examination. Dr. McGrath found that Moll had suffered horrific injuries from at least two gunshot wounds to the head, and had died from shock and haemorrhage. He placed the time of death at between twenty-four and forty-eight hours before 1.15 on Friday (when his examination ended), or at least fifteen hours before his examination. This wide margin of doubt as to the time of death – from 1.50 p.m. on Wednesday, the day Moll was last seen alive, to 9.30 p.m. on Thursday, almost eleven hours after Gleeson called to the police station – was later to prove of crucial significance. Some idea of the extent of the injuries inflicted on Moll may be gleaned from the evidence later given by Dr. McGrath. Her skull had been fractured in several places; her jugular vein had been punctured; her spine had also been fractured. One whole side of her face was missing, from the chin right up to her eye-brow. Pieces of bone and two teeth were found nearly a foot away from the body. Little wonder that, according to friends, Dr. O'Connor became violently ill after his examination of the corpse.

Almost two dozen lead pellets from a shot-gun were found by Dr. McGrath in, on or close to the body. When he moved it, he found several cartridge-wads in the clothes. Moll's neck was peppered with pellet-marks, with one cartridge-wad wedged in her hair. Apart from her coat having been torn, her clothes had not been damaged. The collar had been ripped apart with pellets and, although the coat itself was still buttoned, there was blood on its interior – an odd discovery, whose significance seems to have been overlooked by everybody. Some of Dr. McGrath's other findings and opinions only increased local speculation about the identity of the murderer or murderers. Moll's body had, he believed, been moved after she was felled by the first shot. The artificial position of her legs, with one partly over the other, was, he felt, consistent with the body having been lifted, probably away from the fence. The fact that there were no marks of any struggle suggested that she had been ambushed, or knew her attacker or attackers. Finally, despite the prolonged heavy rain of the previous night, he found the grass and stones under the body dry. That Friday evening Dr. P.J. Stokes of Fethard, the local coroner, opened an inquest in New Inn police station, sitting with a jury, normally chosen at random in such a case. One of the jury, it is believed, was a local retired tailor, Joseph Moloney, who will later figure prominently in this book. Supt. Mahony announced that he would call evidence of identification only, and then seek an adjournment, the usual procedure when a criminal investigation has begun.

Two witnesses gave evidence. Sergeant Anthony Daly from New Inn station (who, with Guard Ruth, had driven Gleeson back to Caesars' the previous morning) identified the body. He said he had known Moll from the previous June and had last seen her alive around 3.30 p.m. on the previous Wednesday. This, it later transpired, was only a few hours before she last left home. Dr. McGrath then summarised his findings and opinions as to the cause of death. In response to the coroner, he offered the view that the body had lain at the spot where it was found for "anything up to ten hours", a finding that has always been regarded locally as highly suspect. Shortly after the inquest Miss Cooney took possession of the body, had it coffined and then arranged for its burial in her own family plot at Garranlea. Some six months earlier she had arranged for Moll's last child to be buried in the same spot. I have been unable to confirm that either body was brought to the local church.

From the day Harry Gleeson had reported his discovery of the body, it appears that someone from the Caesar household, who were, after all, Moll's nearest neighbours, was regarded as a possible suspect by the Guards. Late that afternoon Supt. Mahony and Sergt. James Reynolds called to the house and persuaded Caesar to hand over his gun, some cartridges and a cleaning-rod used with the gun. Within twenty-four hours Caesar, his wife and Tommy Reid had been eliminated. But at 4.00 p.m. the next day (Friday 22 November) two more Guards, Inspector Thomas O'Reilly and Sergt. Matthew Breen, entered Caesar's yard, where they asked Gleeson to accompany them into the sitting-room. There for the next three hours he made a detailed statement. Neither officer administered the customary caution explaining his right to remain silent because, the police later admitted, he was not yet a suspect.

Before the session in the room began, Gleeson asked the inspector if they had fixed the time of Moll's death, to which O'Reilly replied: "I don't know". Asked to account for his movements on the previous morning (Thursday 21 November) Gleeson did so fully. After rising at 8.10 or 8.15 he had, he said, lit a fire and eaten his breakfast. Then with Reid he went out on the farm around 8.50 or 8.55. There they each milked six cows, returning to the house between 9.30 and 9.45. Next, Gleeson continued, he went out to exercise a greyhound, to locate a straying bull and to count sheep. He reached the gap where Moll was lying at about 9.45. Rushing home to announce his discovery, he decided to inform the Guards. Walking by the fields to the village, he arrived there around 10.15 and met Guard Scully. Then with Sergt. Daly and Guard Ruth he returned to the scene, and as they approached the fence one of the Guards asked: "Is it like Molly Carthy?" Gleeson replied: "It looks like her foxy head." Gleeson then outlined his movements on the previous Saturday, Monday and Tuesday, before moving to Wednesday (20 November), the day Moll was last seen by her family. That day his uncle and Mrs. Caesar were in Cashel selling pigs. He spent the morning and afternoon ploughing, finishing at about 5.00 p.m. His uncle returned at 5.30. At 5.45 Harry took his hounds out for exercise, returning at 6.30. He had his supper at 6.45, and then read the daily paper. At 6.30 a neighbour, Willie Ryan, came in, and the four (Gleeson, Ryan and the two Caesars) sat round the fire chatting until about 9.00 p.m. Gleeson then went out to settle the horses for the night, coming in again at about 9.30 to find the two men still sitting by the fire. After a few minutes Gleeson retired to bed, as they had all been up much earlier than usual that day to help with arrangements for the trip into Cashel.

Then, apparently in response to specific questions, Gleeson spoke about Moll. He had known her for at least twelve or thirteen years, as she used to draw water at "our pump". He last saw her alive on Tuesday between 2.30 and 3.00 p.m. some 200 to 300 yards from him in her own field. He never had a conversation with her, except to salute her or to talk to her about her goats trespassing on his uncle's land. He named each of the reputed fathers of her first six children, in some cases giving their past and present addresses and their occupations. Asked if Moll could reach the village by a route that would take her past where she was found, Gleeson said she could, but that it was not a recognised path. He added that an old Mass path existed by the Lynch and Heffernan farms, and he had often seen her go to New Inn that way. At no time on Wednesday did he hear any shots, nor on Thursday morning before he found the body. Asked about any shooting in the area in the previous days, Gleeson said that he had seen nobody shooting on his uncle's land during the week. He had done no shooting himself during the week, nor had anyone lately, and he saw no tinkers or other strangers in the area on Tuesday, Wednesday or Thursday.

Three days later, on Monday 25 November, the Guards – including Supt. Mahony and Inspector O'Reilly, with three other Guards also in attendance – were back in Caesar's house to obtain a second statement from Gleeson. The house was searched and some more cartridges taken; Gleeson's clothes were confiscated and he was given a new suit. Then the three Guards left, leaving the two officers behind. Mahony and O'Reilly went into the sitting-room and told Harry they wanted to take another statement from him. This time they cautioned him. He replied; "I will answer any question and account for my movements; only tell me what you want." That the police meant business on the occasion of this second statement and probably suspected Gleeson of being the murderer is evident from the steps they took to ensure complete privacy during their interrogation. Before the Supt., Inspector and three Guards arrived at Caesar's house, John Caesar and his wife had been collected by a different police party and brought into New Inn police station, where they were kept for most of that day. Neither of the couple ever indicated to friends or to the family solicitor that he or she had made any statement to the Guards; clearly they were simply detained for the day to ensure that, back at Marlhill, the coast was clear for the session with Gleeson.

Nor was this the end of police precautions taken to ensure the privacy at the house. Monday being a day on which Caesar had his milk delivered to the creamery, situated on the main Dublin-Cork road just below the police station, Tommy Reid had just completed his delivery of Caesar's milk at

11.30 and had loaded some skimmed milk and a bag of cattle feeding-stuff on to his ass and cart. As he passed the station on his way home, Guard Frank Gralton (a survivor from the pre-1922 Royal Irish Constabulary) emerged to tell Reid that he "was wanting inside here to give a statement". This veteran of the British administration even tied-up Reid's donkey, almost as if he knew that Reid's visit "inside" might be more than a courtesy call on the new sergeant. There was, sadly, no red carpet laid down for the twenty-six-year-old farm labourer; but at least he was warmly welcomed at the station door by a Chief Superintendent. When he was allowed home 13 hours later (after midnight, the village now being in total darkness) Reid had a black eye and a swollen and discoloured face; a bleeding nose had, he said later, been staunched by Sergt. Daly before he was allowed out. Half a century later, a respected resident of the area, whose veracity I do not doubt, described to me Reid's facial condition as he saw it six days after his interrogation. This agrees with the record kept by Dr. O'Connor of Reid's visit to him at 11.00 a.m. on 26 November: "2-inch abrasion in front of the left ear, consistent with having been struck with a fist". That week Sergt. Daly verbally abused villagers who told him about Reid's injuries. When on 26 November Mrs. Caesar met Supt. Mahony and complained about the treatment Reid had received, the officer's reaction (as recorded by her solicitor) was: "You sometimes have to knock out of a fellow – to knock out of him – what's in".

Gleeson's second statement (like Reid's visit to the Guards) took thirteen hours – from 12.10 p.m. on Monday to 1.10 a.m. on Tuesday. Nearly all of it was taken in the sitting-room, where his local police force had thoughtfully even lit a fire in the grate. During this marathon session there were some adjournments, one at least involving a walk on the lands. There were three breaks for meals, and shorter ones for a smoke. There was also an interruption from a Guard who had been over in Carthy's house. Gleeson began his second statement with personal details – his age, place of birth and duration of residence with his uncle. He said that in the Summer he and Reid slept in an outside loft, moving into a bedroom over the kitchen for the Winter. Asked to explain a stain found on the neck of his shirt, he said the garment had been scorched by heat from a fire after the last Cashel fair. With the rest of his soiled clothes it had, as usual, been laundered by one of two local women, who charged for this work. Asked to account for his movements from the previous Monday, Gleeson insisted on starting with Saturday. He went through all the daily chores – milking cows, walking hounds, inspecting cattle, ploughing, cutting weeds, attending to horses and so on. He had visited a coursing. friend, John Leamy, where he had met another companion, Stephen Barrett. Later he had read the paper, then secured the farm gates, retiring to bed around 10.00 p.m.

Asked about Sunday, Gleeson went into similar details. After Mass he had recovered his uncle's bull. He had spent the day hunting [meaning coursing] at Dogstown with Patrick Coman, Michael Maher and John Leamy. Then they had all gone to Michael Barron's house at Belleview, where they had remained until 11.30 p.m. Turning to Monday, Gleeson once more described the familiar routine of farm and domestic chores, before he had gone out to resume the ploughing he had been at on Saturday. After his evening meal he had read the paper until 9 o'clock, then retired after securing the stock and gates. On Tuesday he was at a water-pump on his uncle's land between 2.00 and 2.30 when he saw Moll Carthy in the distance, spancelling goats on her land. A neighbour, Mrs. Thomas Ryan, had arrived at his uncle's house on a visit before he went out on the land. That afternoon he had done more ploughing, but had to stop because of the rain. He then did some fencing until it got dark. Next he had visited a neighbour, John Halpin, who had given him a newspaper. Gleeson said he read only about sports and dogs, leaving the rest of the paper to Caesar and his wife, who divided the pages between them. He then went in some detail through his movements on Wednesday 20 November. As the lorry to collect the pigs was due at 9.00 a.m., he had risen before 7.00 a.m. to get through his usual chores, so as to be ready to assist in loading the pigs. "The boss" went in the lorry with the pigs; later it transpired that Mrs. Caesar had followed in the pony-and-trap.

On Wednesday afternoon, Gleeson said, he had ploughed for two hours, finishing at 5.00 p.m. Asked if he had been near the Dug-Out (close to where the body was found, and where the Guards believed Moll had been killed), Harry said he had had occasion to go near it once before he began to plough, to release a sheep that had become entangled in briars. When he came home Reid was around the house, but went out about 5.15 to milk the cows. Around 6.30 the two Caesars returned in the trap from Cashel. Harry then went out to exercise the hounds, returning to join the Caesars and Reid for supper. After the meal he had read the "Independent"; he thought it was around 7.00 p.m. when he started to read, about 30 minutes after Willie Ryan arrived. He recalled Ryan being teased by Caesar about "a foxy girl" he had recently met at a local dance. Around 9.00 p.m. Gleeson took the lamp and went out to secure the horses. On his return he joined the company around the fire, retiring to bed around 9.30. Next Gleeson dealt in detail with the events of Thursday, the day he walked to the police station. He had breakfasted with Reid and then helped him with the cows. Noticing that the bull had strayed again, he went in search of it and found it. Then with his hound he had entered the Dug-Out Field to count the ewes in the adjoining field. At this stage he had caught up his dog, as he could not allow it to continue loose, lest it should worry the sheep. When he was partly up on the gap and about to enter the ploughed field he heard a dog growl, and saw a small black dog and a woman lying alongside it. He hurried back to the Caesars, who were in their bedroom; after he had told them about the woman, he decided to go to the Guards. The body was in the same position when he returned with them. He did not wait long enough to recognise Moll, even though he admitted when pressed that he had recognised her 200 yards off on the Tuesday. On Thursday she was either sleeping or dead; he did not notice anything wrong with her head.

When he returned with the two Guards, Sergt. Daly said: "It's Moll Carthy". Gleeson said: "God, it must be; look at the foxy head". He had known her about sixteen years. He used to tell her to take light branches of firewood when cut, and she had often got water in the field at Caesar's house. A month earlier Reid was "flogging" her goats out of a field when her son Michael, then about twelve, arrived and threatened to get the Guards. His interrogators now asked Gleeson about giving Moll potatoes. He said that about two years earlier he had given her some, throwing them over her fence at dusk. Neither his uncle or aunt knew about this. He had not spoken to Moll on the previous Tuesday; he did not get a bag from her that day to hold potatoes, which he would give her the next day when his uncle was away with the pigs. He had made no appointment on Tuesday to meet Moll at the Dug-Out on Wednesday with the potatoes.

In reply to questions, Gleeson said Moll had never suggested he was the father of her last child; nor had he ever heard that she had said so. He had never met her late at night; she usually had one of her boys with her if she went to the village late at night. He had last spoken to her about three weeks or a month earlier, when he had had a few words with her about her goats, when her son Michael was with her. Asked about his uncle's gun, Gleeson said he had last used it at harvest time. He had never cleaned it. It was kept in "the boss's" bedroom and would have been there on the previous Wednesday and Thursday. Finally he said he had discussed Moll's death only with Reid, advising him the day he found the body to tell the Guards the truth and everything he knew.

One does not need to be a criminal lawyer or even a reader of crime novels to realise the case the Guards could make against Gleeson from this statement. In the course of a friendship, of a nature that could easily be hinted at in the circumstances, he had occasionally supplied Moll with potatoes and firewood without his uncle's knowledge. When the pair met on the Tuesday they had agreed to meet again on the Wednesday while the two Caesars were away, when he would return her a bag she had given him on Tuesday, now filled with potatoes. At this second meeting at dusk he had, it would be alleged, killed her, and the next morning he had "discovered" her body. As to the motive Gleeson might have for murdering Moll Carthy, one had already been supplied to the Guards by one of her sons, who had also probably told them of the alleged tryst at the Dug-Out. Moll, a son claimed, had accused Harry of fathering her seventh child, and had threatened to expose him. Should the Caesars be convinced, so the police theory ran, that an immoral relationship had existed, Harry's prospects of inheriting the farm would be gone. Accordingly, he had had to kill her.

On Saturday 30 November, five days after giving his second statement, Harry Gleeson was arrested at his uncle's home and brought to New Inn police station. There he was charged by Supt. Mahony with the murder of Moll Carthy. His reply was that he had no "hand, act or part" in it, and he asked the Supt. to repeat the times within which the crime was alleged to have been committed. When Mahony did so, Gleeson commented: "Right, I can account for my movements; ye have ye'er duty". Later that day, at a special court in Cashel police station, Mr. Francis Phillips, a peace commissioner, formally remanded Gleeson in custody to Fethard District Court on the following Friday, 6 December. When asked if he had anything to say, Gleeson replied: "No, sir, whatever statement I gave, I gave". He was then brought to Limerick jail, some 40 miles away.

Although now in custody on a charge that carried the death penalty if he was convicted, Gleeson still had no professional advice. As if only now realising the gravity of his situation, his family moved fast to get him a lawyer. That evening John J. Timoney, a solicitor practising in Tipperary town, visited the Caesars. On Monday 2 December he travelled to Limerick jail, where he met Gleeson for the first time and was formally instructed by him to defend him. A week later on 9 December Timoney went by train to Dublin, where he met Sean MacBride, who accepted the brief as junior counsel for Gleeson. At Fethard District Court on 6 December Timoney appeared for Gleeson; the local State solicitor Frank O'Connor was for the prosecution. Gleeson was remanded to Cahir District Court for 19 December. On that day MacBride opposed a request for a further adjournment. District Justice Troy – he who, coincidentally, had some years before refused to commit the Carthy children to State care – fixed 2 January 1941 as the date on which the depositions stage would commence at a special sitting, adding that there would be no more adjournments.

Between Harry Gleeson's arrest on 30 November and the start of the full District Court hearing on 2 January, the Guards were very busy. Some of their activities strike one as somewhat unorthodox. On Sunday December 1 Gleeson's solicitor met Supt. Mahony in Cahir Garda station. Mahony said that a local auctioneer, Patrick Maher, was a relative of Mrs. Caesar and that, as a relative of Maher and a local solicitor, he (Mahony) was surprised that anyone other than that legal firm would act for the Caesars. Timoney's reaction is not recorded. The following day (Monday 2 December), while Timoney and John Caesar were in Limerick visiting Gleeson in jail there, an absence from home by Caesar that would have been known to the local Guards, Supt. Mahony called on Mrs Caesar at her home. His manner was friendly, even condescending. Suddenly he asked: "Did he [Timoney] come looking for the case? Generally these fellows do". Then, in more explicit terms than he had used the day before to Timoney, he suggested that the Caesars should change solicitors and employ Maher & Co. of Cahir. Nor was this the end of unorthodox police activity before the trial began. Some days later three Guards, Inspector O'Reilly, Detective Sergt. Vaughan and Guard Scully, called on Patrick Furlong, a neighbour and close friend, and a relative of Mrs. Caesar. They too brought up the subject of Timoney acting for Gleeson, and asked Furlong about Timoney's visits to Caesar's home. Furlong naturally reported this visit to the Caesars, who told Timoney.

Timoney went at once to Cahir police station to complain to Mahony about these two visits, and about what he felt was improper pressure on him to give up the case. Not finding the Supt. at the station, he went to the officer's home, where he complained strongly to Mahony about his and his mens' action. Not apparently knowing of the police call on Furlong, the Supt. assured Timoney that the three Guards had had no authority from him for their visit. By now Timoney was also acting for Tommy Reid, who (on the advice of Fr. O'Malley) had asked to see Timoney on his next visit to Caesars'. He told him of the beating he said he had got in the police station on 25 November when "called in" for interview. While he was in Mahony's house Timoney also mentioned this alleged assault. The Supt.'s reaction was curious. First he pointed out that he was away on the day in question, implying that he neither knew of nor had authorised any rough treatment of Reid. He then added that from his own enquiries (showing that he had already heard of Reid's allegation) he did not accept Reid's story. His information, he told Timoney, was that it was Gleeson who had beaten up Reid after the latter "had said certain things in my station". How he heard of the alleged assault on Reid was not disclosed.

Outside Fethard courthouse on 6 December Timoney had a brief meeting with Chief Supt. Reynolds. Faced with an even more senior officer than Mahony, but not yet realising that Reynolds was one of the two officers Reid had said had assaulted him, Timoney brought up Reid's complaint. Reynolds' reaction was that, if anything illegal had happened, there would be "no shielding". He admitted to Timoney that one of the detectives in the McCarthy case, Detective Sergt. Vaughan (one of the recent visitors to Furlong) had recently got off on a technicality in a prosecution for assaulting a witness. He also told Timoney of another recent case where the complainant had dropped the charge because, he believed, the Guards involved would perjure themselves. In the course of their investigations into the murder, two detectives visited Feehan's hardware store in Cashel, where most of the ammunition used in the New Inn area was purchased. They inspected the firearms register and pointed out to the staff that it contained no record of any sale to John Caesar, on a date they mentioned, of cartridges of a type they also mentioned. As they left, they said threateningly to the staff that on their next visit they expected to find such an entry in the register.

Map used in the case of The People -v- Gleeson. Redrawn from original made by Guard Wm. J. Quinlan, 6 Dec., 1940.

Chapter 3

A case to answer

Depositions in the case of The People versus Henry Gleeson took six days in January 1941 in Clonmel District Court. The hearings were spread over three weeks. During the first week the court sat on three days, in the second week on two days and in the third on one day. As at the preliminary hearing in December, the presiding judge was District Justice Troy. Appearing for the State was George Murnaghan BL, then a junior counsel of ten years' standing, and later for 25 years a High Court judge. The charge against Gleeson was that between 5.00 p.m. on (Wednesday) 20 November 1940 and 10.20 a.m. on (Thursday) 21 November 1940 he murdered Mary McCarthy. In his opening address Murnaghan outlined the facts he would be relying on. Mary McCarthy, he stated, had left home around 6.30 p.m. on Wednesday 20 November 1940. Around 7.00 p.m. two shots were heard coming from the area where her body was later found. The State would prove she had been killed by two gun-shot wounds to the head. The evidence of about fifty witnesses would, Murnaghan concluded, connect the accused man with the crime. Actually forty-eight witnesses were called. Twenty were mainly local people; no fewer than twenty-six more were Guards.

Guard Joseph Ruth of New Inn station, the first witness, said that on Thursday 21 November he went with Gleeson and Sergeant Daly to Marlhill. Before that he had seen Gleeson in the station, where in Glesson's presence Guard Scully (also of New Inn station) had said to Ruth: "Harry is after finding a woman dead in Caesar's field". Gleeson said he had been out counting sheep; he had dogs with him getting them ready for coursing. He looked across the ditch and saw her lying there; a small black dog on the body growled at him. Sergeant Daly then came in, Ruth continued, and the three of them – Daly, Ruth and Gleeson – left immediately in Daly's car. On the way Ruth asked Gleeson if it was anybody from the locality; Gleeson said he didn't know. Daly asked if she was dead; Gleeson said "she may be sleeping". Ruth then asked Gleeson if he knew who owned the dog; Gleeson said he didn't. Gleeson's demeanour was "quite normal". Ruth then described finding the body, lying on its back close to the ditch with a small black dog on it. He recognised Mary McCarthy from eight yards away; he had last seen her the previous Monday. The sergeant caught up the dog and handed it to Gleeson; both then left. About fifteen minutes later Gleeson returned. Ruth told him not to cross by the gap, saying he didn't want any marks left or anything disturbed. Gleeson came that way "all the same", remarking: "I suppose I done wrong; it can't be helped; they are my marks anyway". He had brought back a sheet, which they used to cover the body; then Gleeson left, this time by the gate. Later Superintendent Mahony and a local priest, Father Denis Blackburn, arrived. The State Pathologist did not arrive until the next morning.

Michael McCarthy, the second eldest son of the dead woman, and probably the most important witness in the whole case, was next to take the stand. He told the judge he was twelve-and-a-half. Although the court hearing must have been traumatic for a boy of his age, he broke down only once. Stating that he lived with his mother, brothers and sisters, Michael said they had seven goats, one donkey and two dogs. One of the dogs, a small black and white one, they had for only six weeks; this was presumably the dog found near his mother's body. Asked first about Tuesday (19 November), the day before the day his mother went missing, Michael said he was at school. So was his sister Nellie. They got out at about four o'clock and were home by five. Mary, Biddy and Connie were there; his mother was not. She was out gathering firewood and came in later. Nellie and he got their own dinners – tea and bread, as there were no potatoes. His mother got back "not long after it got dark". Then Nellie went to Condon's, a neighbouring farm, for milk; after that they all had supper together. His mother went out around seven o'clock. Here he broke down. He did not know what time she came back because he was in bed.

On Wednesday (20 November), the day he last saw his mother alive, Michael said, he was not at school, but stayed around the yard. Sergeant Daly came to the house that day, but nobody else. His mother did not go out that night after tea; he last saw her alive about seven or eight o'clock. She went down through the fields about three-quarters of an hour after tea. A few minutes after she left he cycled to Condon's to get milk. Jim Condon had been to McCarthys' earlier with a goat after Michael came home from school. When Condon left, Michael had his dinner; there were no potatoes in the house that day either. He saw Mr. and Mrs. Caesar return in their trap before his dinner. His brother Paddy came in later from work; Michael didn't know at what time. Asked about Thursday (21 November), Michael said that after breakfast he went down towards the Dug-Out Field. He saw Harry Gleeson beside it on top of a ditch; he had a hound with him. When he saw Michael he jumped down; Michael then ran home.

In reply to Murnaghan, the boy tried to explain the relationship between his mother and Gleeson. There was, he said, a pump in one of Caesar's fields where the McCarthys drew water; the Caesars also used it. When he was with his mother he often met Harry there. Moll and Harry used to stop there; he would go home; his mother would tell him to go. She would come home a good while after; he never looked back to see what they were doing. They would be going along the side of the ditch; he saw them there a "good couple of times". Once he saw Harry wave to Moll; Harry was then at the pump and she was in her house. She came out to meet Harry; Michael didn't know if they went anywhere; she would be a long time away. Once he saw Harry wave from a shed, but he stopped when he saw Michael. In May his mother had a baby who lived only three weeks. She told him who the father was. About a month later their goat went into Caesar's field. Harry came along; Moll and Harry were "fighting". He didn't know what it was about, but she told Gleeson she would "put him up to law to pay for the child". He didn't hear Gleeson say anything; he wasn't near enough to hear. After that they continued to meet. One day Harry was doing fencing and Moll was talking to him. The two Caesars came along in their trap. He heard Gleeson say: "Here they are now; go in". He once saw Harry looking out of a shed door for Moll; he might have a bag of spuds for her. They used to get spuds from the Halpins, but not from the Caesars. One night his mother sent him out to the fields with Paddy. On a ditch they found "a butt of spuds" in their bag. He saw his mother bring home spuds more than once.

Michael remembered Detective Wall bringing him to Caesar's house, where Sergeant Kelly showed him a lot of potato bags. He looked through them and saw their bag amongst them; he had last seen it at his house the week his mother died. He remembered Superintendent Mahony coming to his house with Harry Gleeson; Harry was looking for a potato-bag. "I said something to Harry as he left; I don't remember what I said.... I don't know if what I said was friendly or not". Just what Michael (and Paddy too) said that day to Gleeson, according to the Superintendent, will be told later. It was distinctly unfriendly. Later in this book an attempt will be made to reconstruct the movements of both Moll and Harry from Tuesday 19 November to Thursday 21 November, and the role of Michael McCarthy will be analysed. At this stage some apparent discrepancies in the evidence of this boy, not yet into his teens, might be pointed out. Some of these inconsistencies were noticed by New Inn folk in court. Michael said that Sergeant Daly called to his home on Wednesday, but nobody else, that his mother did not go out after tea that day, and that Condon came with a goat after Michael came from school. Clearly Daly was not the only caller that day; Condon called also. Clearly his mother did go out after tea. And how could Condon come with a goat after Michael came from school, since Michael said he wasn't at school that day? What local people in court did not know is that the local school-roll, which I have inspected, shows that Michael did attend school on the Wednesday.

The most astonishing evidence Michael gave related to the probable time his mother died. The State alleged that she died between 5.00 p.m. on Wednesday and 10.20 a.m. on Thursday; Murnaghan had said she left home around 6.30 and was killed around 7.00 p.m. Yet Michael said he last saw his mother "at 7 or 8 o'clock" on Wednesday evening. The State's purpose in putting Michael in the witness box was probably two-fold. First, he would suggest the existence of an improper relationship between Gleeson and his mother, thus helping to create a motive for the murder. Secondly, he would suggest the existence of a secret arrangement between his mother and Gleeson regarding the handing over of potatoes to Moll. This would explain Michael's story of finding McCarthy's sack in Caesar's house, and his evidence of previous furtive gifts of potatoes from Gleeson to his mother. It would also suggest a reason for a secret meeting between Gleeson and his mother.

After Michael the stand was taken by Thomas Reid, the other live-in employee at Caesar's. He said he had worked for Caesar for nine years, and remembered the day in November when Caesar's pigs were brought to Cashel. They were taken by lorry and Caesar accompanied them. The lorry left between 1 and 2 p.m.; about half or three-quarters of an hour later, Mrs. Caesar followed in the trap. When the Caesars left, Reid was alone in the house; after a while Harry came in and they dined together. Then Harry ploughed the field beside the Dug-Out Field, returning at about 5.15, when Reid milked the cows. The next time he saw Gleeson was around 7.00 p.m., just as Reid stood up from his supper. The table had been set for four, and the two Caesars sat down as Reid left and Gleeson came in. Reid told the judge he came in from the cows around 6.15; from then until he finished his tea he did not see Gleeson around the house. This still left the period between 6.15 and 7.00 for which Reid could not confirm any account Gleeson might give of his movements then. On the following day (Thursday 21 November), Reid said he remembered when the body was found, but he "disremembered" whether or not Gleeson had mentioned to him whose body it was, either then or at any time before his arrest. During the previous Summer Mary McCarthy used to come to Caesar's house [meaning the yard] for water. The last time he saw her doing so was after he heard she had had a baby. The day her body was found Harry brought back a dog to Caesar's house. He gave it to Reid, who saw blood on its paws. Gleeson that day was in his "everyday clothes". Harry always wore a cap, but he could not recall him wearing an overcoat, only a raincoat. Reid only knew Moll to see. In the evenings he was in the habit of going out after tea instead of remaining in the house.

26

Mary McCarthy, at nineteen the oldest of Moll's surviving children, substantially confirmed Michael's account of the events of Tuesday 19 November. She, it transpired, had accompanied her mother that afternoon to collect firewood. It was just dark when they reached home. Then with her younger sister Nellie she went to Condon's for the milk; on their return all five had supper together. Some time after 6.00 p.m. her mother went out. Mary could not recall when Moll returned, but all the family were then in bed. On Wednesday (20 November), Mary stated, Michael and Nellie were at school. That day she had lunch with her mother and Connie – tea, bread and butter, as there were no potatoes. Mary remembered Michael and Nellie coming from school, then their neighbour Condon arriving with his goat, and after that Michael and Nellie having dinner. Her mother sat at the fire during this meal and later had her own supper. Then Moll secured some goats and left through Caesar's fields. She was followed by Michael for a short distance; the black dog went too. It was just getting dark, but Mary could not say what time it was.

Finally, Mary dealt (more briefly than Michael) with the relationship between her mother and Gleeson. She had seen them standing in the back field. Sometimes she would leave and they would stay; sometimes her mother would come home after a short time, but on other occasions after " a good while". She last saw them talking together "around the holiday before her mother went away", presumably 1 November. On at least three matters Mary's evidence differed from Michael's. First, she said she had accompanied her mother on Tuesday gathering firewood; if (as Michael had said) Moll was not at home when he came in from school, neither was Mary, contrary to what he had stated. Secondly, according to Mary, she had accompanied Nellie to Condon's for the milk; Michael said only Nellie had gone. More important was Mary's evidence that Michael had been at school on Wednesday; he had said he had spent the day around the yard.

Patrick McCarthy, Moll's eldest son, then fifteen-and-a-half, was the next witness. He could give no evidence about Tuesday 19 November because for the previous few months he had been working and sleeping at Hanley's, a local farm. He usually called home each evening to see his mother, but did not do so on Tuesday because he had met her that day while she was out gathering firewood. On Wednesday (20 November), Patrick said, he arrived home around 8.15 p.m. Everybody was there except his mother. After Michael told him something (presumably about his mother's departure), and as it was then raining, he went out to a shed first and later (probably when the rain stopped) down to the field beside the Dug-Out Field. He saw nothing; he stopped and listened in the dark for five minutes. With his sister Mary he sat up till 2.00 a.m.; then both retired. The following morning (Thursday 21 November) he rose at

8.00 a.m. and left for work. Asked about Gleeson, he said he had seen him "keeping company" with his mother. He knew Harry used to give his mother potatoes. He told of the birth the previous May of a sister, who died after three weeks. His mother told him the father's identity. Finally, Patrick confirmed Michael's story about being sent out one night to a fence, where they found a bag of theirs full of potatoes. He gave no evidence of the occasion (described by Michael) when Supt. Mahony showed them potato bags in Caesar's premises, although it later transpired that Patrick had been present too. On two points Patrick's evidence merits comment. He said that Sergt. Daly had called to his house on Tuesday. Although this may have been an error for Wednesday, it adds to the unsolved mystery of Daly's visit. He also said his search on Wednesday night for his mother was made alone; according to Michael, he had gone with Patrick.

Three local men next gave evidence. Martin Vokes, a carpenter and a nephew of Gleeson, said he had twice worked the previous year at Caesar's. Caesar had a single-barrelled gun, which he allowed Vokes to use. After he had been out shooting crows, Caesar used to leave it by the end of the kitchen dresser. On Tuesday 19 November Vokes was in the house a third time, staying all day. He didn't see the gun that day; Gleeson might have mentioned to him about a fox in the high field; Gleeson "might have said anything". William Ryan said that, when working from July to Christmas 1940 for a farmer named Fitzgerald in Marlhill, he often visited Caesar's at night. He would leave around 10.30 or 11.00 p.m. Often Gleeson was not there in the evenings; he would be out walking his dogs and would not have gone to bed before Ryan left. On the night before Moll Carthy's body was found, Ryan remembered Gleeson going to bed before Ryan left around 10.30. That night Harry was out of the house, but not for long. He came in once with a hound to feed and went out again to put in a pony. Ryan also remembered Mrs. Caesar offering Harry tea; he declined, saying he was tired of drinking that day. Mrs. Caesar remarked that they were all tired as they had been up early, a reference to the pig-sale in Cashel. Ryan said he had twice seen Gleeson with a shot-gun. In Caesar's on the night of 23 November Mrs. Caesar spoke of Moll's death and Gleeson told of finding the body. He had been out walking a dog; as he went along the side of the ditch he looked over and saw the body. He went towards her, but got frightened and did not go too far. Harry said he had told the Guards that from the clothes it might be Moll.

Although Thomas Hennessy, the next witness, had little to say, it was vital to the State case. On Wednesday 20 November he left his home at Knockillen near New Inn around 6.30 p.m. to cycle to the village. It was then dark, a fine but windy night. To reach the road to New Inn he had to cross five fields. When he was in the fourth he heard a shot behind him from the north, then after two or three seconds a second shot from the same direction. No other witness corroborated Hennessy's story. He was followed in the witness box by the State Pathologist and six Guards. Two of the latter were Guard William Quinlan and Superintendent Daniel Stapleton, both from police headquarters. Quinlan was a mapping expert and Stapleton a ballistics expert. Quinlan described measurements, on maps he had drawn of the area where the body lay, made under Supt. Mahony's supervision. Other maps were based on information given to him by Hennessy, the only person who had heard the two shots. Quinlan said that when Hennessy heard the first shot he was about three-quarters of a mile from the fence near where the body was found.

Supt. Stapleton said that the first shot that struck Moll Carthy was fired from five or six feet. The second, which caused an extensive neck wound and blew her face away, was fired with the gun-muzzle held close to her at the moment of firing. He had been given, by the Guard in charge of State exhibits in the case, a single-barrelled 12-bore breech-loaded American shot-gun and a cleaning-rod for use with it. In the immediate vicinity of the apparent location of the crime he had found a large number of wads and spent cartridges. Alcoholic tests indicated that two wads could have been fired on or about 22 November. He could not fix a precise date because of the effects of weather on the wads. All the wads and cartridges had come from the same lot and had been fired from the same gun.

The evidence of the State Pathologist, Dr John McGrath, was crucial to the prosecution case. A summary of his findings and views have already been given in Chapter 2; he also gave detailed evidence at the subsequent trial. Moll Carthy in Dr. McGrath's opinion died within 24 to 48 hours before 1.50 p.m. on Friday 22 November; this view was based on the body temperature. An alternative time of death, at least fifteen hours before his examination (on 22 November) before, was based on the fact that rigor mortis had set in by then. He believed that death had occurred within two to five hours after the ingestion of the food found in the dead woman's stomach. The time of her last meal was, however, never ascertained. Dr. McGrath said that on 27 November he had been given by the Guards items of men' clothing, clearly those of Gleeson. He had examined them for traces of human blood; he had found it on some of them, but not to any significant extent.

Michael Gayson, a farm labourer, told the court that in June 1940 he had spent a fortnight plastering Caesar's house. While there he saw a gun beside the kitchen dresser. He had seen Gleeson, Vokes and Caesar use it; cartridges for it were kept near the fireplace. John Halpin said he had two farms, one adjacent to Caesar's. Moll Carthy lived in a small house near his land; her family had been there for fifty years. He remembered meeting

Gleeson the previous May after the birth of her last child. Gleeson asked him if he had heard of "an occurrence a little further down the way". Halpin said he hadn't and was surprised; he asked Gleeson who was responsible, but Harry didn't know. Halpin said he had noticed the Carthys recently using a pump in Caesar's field; before that they used to go to his yard and use a pump there. Moll would be at the pump in the field when Gleeson was there, so he advised Harry that if he could get her to resume using the pump in Caesar's yard, he would not run the risk of being associated with her. On Wednesday (19 November), the day before Moll's body was found, Gleeson came to his house around 11.00 a.m.. On the Tuesday night he had also been there with two dogs, looking for a newspaper, and Halpin gave him one. The previous Friday (15 November) Halpin met Gleeson in a passage at the Cow Gate, with a bucket of milk in one hand and a gun in the other. The gun seemed newly-oiled; he never saw it clean before. Gleeson said he might meet the fox; he had seen one pulling a goose.

James Condon said that Moll Carthy kept a goat for stud purposes. On Wednesday 20 November he went to her house around 5.30 p.m. where he met her son Michael. At about 7.00 p.m. that evening Michael came to his house for milk. William Fitzgerald remembered the morning the body was found. Between 12.30 and 12.45 he was carting manure near Caesar's house when Caesar and his wife came out and told him about the body. Gleeson came along, and Fitzgerald said to him: "You are an iron man". Harry replied: "If I had heart disease I was dead". Fitzgerald asked him if there were any tracks. Gleeson said: "No, myself and Guard Ruth searched and you'd think it was easy, as Moll had different [meaning odd] boots". Dr. McGrath had confirmed this. Frank Lenehan said he passed the Carthy house at 8.55 a.m. on Thursday 21 November. It was "full daylight". He saw Michael McCarthy on top of a fence looking towards Caesar's. He had never seen the boy doing this before, " except possibly in the Summer". Eight more Guards next gave evidence, most of it of a technical nature. One of them, Detective Sergeant Breen, told of finding a footprint the day the body was found, close to where it lay. This print fitted a shoe that had been produced earlier, and Breen saw a Guard Moran make a cast of the print. Moran confirmed this. Guard Ruth now returned to the stand, to tell more about where the body lay. When they reached the location, Gleeson hung back seven or eight feet off and said nothing. Ruth denied that Gleeson (contrary to what William Fitzgerald had sworn) had searched with him for footprints or other clues. Michael Leamy, an employee of Feehan's hardware store in Cashel, told of the purchase by John Caesar on 3 October of a box of 25 cartridges. He could not say what type Caesar bought; he usually got No. 4 or 5.

Timothy Halley, a farmer, said he worked for Caesar for three years and saw Caesar's gun a few times. It was kept in the kitchen dresser, but when the Caesars went to town they might put it in their room. Guard Vincent Scully of New Inn, the first person to meet Gleeson in the station on Thursday 21 November, told of Harry's arrival. He told Scully of finding a woman in Caesar's field near the Dug-Out; asked if she was dead, Gleeson replied: "Well, she's lying there anyway". Sergeant Daly came down from his upstairs office; Guard Gralton was there too. Asked by Daly what happened, Gleeson repeated what he had said to Scully, and Daly went for his car. On Monday 25 November at Caesar's Gleeson handed over his clothes and Scully gave him a new suit. Dr. James O'Connor next took the stand. He had been called out by the Guards the morning Gleeson found the body. O'Connor, like Dr. McGrath, found the left leg crossed over the right, implying that this position surprised him, as it had McGrath. He found the dead woman's clothes dry and carefully arranged; there was no disorder, only the collar of the coat being disarranged. Rigor mortis was complete. But, Dr. O'Connor said, he wished to qualify this. He had placed his hand on the body under the clothes and formed the impression that it was warmer than it should have been in the weather conditions. He got a reading of 96 degrees Fahrenheit. Here at the end of his evidence Dr. O'Connor touched on one of the unsolved mysteries of the case.

Sergeant Anthony Daly, one of the key figures in the case, said that on Thursday morning 21 November he came down from his office and met the accused man, who told him of his discovery of the body. Gleeson said he did not know her; she wore a blue dress and "may not be dead". Daly could not give an opinion about Gleeson's demeanour; he had not known him previously. In the car he asked Gleeson if it was a person from the locality. Gleeson said he did not go near her, that he did not know her or the dog, and that she might only be sleeping. When they got nearer the body Daly recognised it from about six yards' distance. He told Gleeson to take the dog; as he didn't do so, Daly himself handed it to Gleeson, sending him for a sheet. Daly returned about 11.40 and asked Gleeson if there was a ram in the field, and if it would attack a person. Gleeson said there was, but it would not attack. He asked Gleeson if the bull was cross, and Gleeson said "No". When Daly first recognised the body he made no remark about its identity. He was stationed in New Inn only from the previous June 25, and last saw Moll Carthy around 3.30 on Wednesday afternoon. He offered no explanation of the circumstances of this contact, nor of where it occurred; none was sought by Murnaghan. Sergeant William Kelly, the Guard in charge of exhibits, said that on Monday 25

November he searched Caesar's house for a sack, which he now identified. It was with thirteen others in Caesar's barn; some were similar, some of the same brand, and all were grain sacks. When he located the one now in court he replaced it with all the others and brought in Michael McCarthy, asking him to pick out any sack he recognised. Michael picked the sack in court. Kelly sent for Superintendent Mahony, who mixed the fourteen sacks in the yard. Twice more they repeated this procedure, asking Michael to select any sack he knew, and each time the boy picked out the same sack.

Superintendent Patrick Mahony of Cahir, the officer in charge of case, said that on Thursday 21 November he went with Guard Gralton to the Caesar farm. They met Gleeson in the yard and asked him for directions to the body; he sent Thomas Reid with them. He then spent twenty minutes at the spot where the body lay, returning at 3.00 p.m. with a lorry-cover, which he used to cover the whole area where the body was. That day John Caesar handed him his gun with cartridges. The following Monday (25 November) Mahony went with Inspector O'Reilly to Caesar's home, where he told Gleeson he would like to search the house and surrounding area for clues. "Search away", said Gleeson, who volunteered to hand over his clothes. Later Mahony cautioned Gleeson orally, and said to him that if there was any bag in the place belonging to the Carthys, he should hand it over. "There is no bag here belonging to the Carthys", Gleeson replied. Mahony was then called away by Sergeant Kelly for the experiment with the sacks with Michael McCarthy. The superintendent said he took from Gleeson the statement of 25 November, and then commenced to read it in court. Sean MacBride now objected to this, arguing that parts of the statement constituted improper cross-examination. District Justice Troy admitted the statement, ruling that on the whole it appeared to be permissable and was a matter for the trial judge. After Gleeson had finished his statement, he told Mahony that a sack had been taken from a pump on his uncle's land three or four weeks earlier; he only noticed it missing the previous Tuesday (19 November). (It was then usual to wrap sacking round pumps in frosty weather). On Tuesday 26 November the Superintendent went with Gleeson to the Carthy home to see if Gleeson could locate the missing sack. Patrick and Michael were there, having been specially brought there by the Guards. The following conversation then took place, according to Mahony – the only person to give evidence of this vital exchange.

> "Paddy: What are you looking for Harry?
> Michael: What are you looking for Harry?
> Harry: A bag that was taken off the pump.
> Michael: What about the bag my mother gave you on Tuesday?
> Harry: I got no bag from your mother on Tuesday.

Michael:	(Pointing his finger at Harry) You did, you did, you did....
Harry:	Tuesday evening – what time?
Michael:	Didn't she tell me she gave you a bag some time on Tuesday.
Harry:	She told you – I wasn't speaking to your mother high or dry on Tuesday.
Michael:	You were; she gave you a bag and don't be telling lies. You were to give her potatoes in it near the Dug-Out on Wednesday night.
Harry:	I wasn't speaking to your mother on Tuesday. I saw her about half-one. She was spancelling goats in the field.
Michael:	She did give you the bag, and she went out on Wednesday night to get potatoes from you, because you were to give them to her while the old people were in Cashel or somewhere; and you are the father of the last child too.
Harry:	Who can prove that?
Paddy:	You are the father of the last child Harry. My mother told me.
Harry:	People could tell lies. Your mother could be telling you things and it might be other people.
Michael:	You are the father of the last child.You were, you were, you were.
Harry:	Had I ever an angry word with you, Sonnie?
Paddy:	You had not.
Michael:	No; but you had with my mother, when she said you were the father of the last child.
Harry:	Who is to prove that?
Paddy:	My mother said it.
Harry:	Did I ever take out a knife to you,Mickey?
Michael:	You did, over near the boreen.
Harry:	Did I open it?
Michael:	You did, and you followed me with it;and you said you would cut off my head.
Harry:	That was when you were young. 'Twas a joke.
Paddy:	You followed him with a knife alright.
Michael:	You were the father of the last child.You're letting on not to be. You needn't be laughing.
Harry:	(To Paddy) Didn't I get rabbits from you?
Paddy:	You did.
Harry:	Didn't I pay you for them?

Paddy:	You did.
Michael:	My mother said you were the father of the last child. You can't deny it.
Harry:	She could tell you many a thing.
Michael:	She did, and you told her to keep her mouth shut about it. You can hit me now for saying it if you like, but you're afraid.
Harry:	Did I ever hit you?
Michael:	You did. She gave you the bag last Tuesday and I saw it above in the house yesterday.
Harry:	There is no bag belonging to you,above, but if you think there is, go up and get it. I never got a bag from your mother.
Michael:	You did, and you were to give her potatoes in it on Wednesday night.
Harry:	(To Paddy) Did you ever see me giving potatoes to your mother?
Paddy:	I often did.
Harry:	What about all the potatoes that were taken out of the pits?
Paddy:	Do you remember the night my mother and myself were down at the snares? You took her down the field for them.You told me to stay where I was, and when she came back she had a butt of potatoes. You often gave herpotatoes. You often gave her potatoes.
Harry:	Your mother was a liar – The Lord have mercy on her soul
Supt:	Molly is dead; better not be talking like that about her.
Michael:	She is dead......"

At this stage, according to Supt. Mahony, he ended the confrontation, as Michael had begun to cry. He was not sure if any other Guards witnessed this scene, but admitted that at least one was inside the McCarthy house. Finally Mahony said he arrested Gleeson at Caesar's on 30 November. When charged with the murder, Gleeson asked him: "What time did you say?" Mahony repeated: "Between 5.00 p.m. on 20 November and 10.20 a.m. on 21 November". Gleeson replied: "Right, I can account for my movements. Ye have to do ye'er duty". The last State witness was Inspector Thomas O'Reilly, who told of writing down Gleeson's first statement. He did not caution him because he was not yet a suspect. O'Reilly confirmed Mahony's evidence that it was after signing his second statement on 25 November that Gleeson told of the bag missing from the pump. When the State case closed, Sean MacBride announced that he did not propose to call evidence. He said he had refrained from cross-examining State witnesses because he felt it was in the best interests of his client to reserve cross-examination for "another court". However, he now submitted that Gleeson had no case to meet and should not be sent for trial. The prosecution evidence, he argued, was at most circumstantial and no direct evidence had been given connecting Gleeson with the crime.

District Justice Troy had no hesitation in reaching a decision. Although, he said, they had heard only one side of the case, he was satisfied the State had made a case against Gleeson. He ordered him to be sent for trial by the Central Criminal Court, and he asked Gleeson if he had anything to say. "I had neither hand, act or part in it", Gleeson answered. As he left the court building he passed a friend from New Inn. "They'd hang you with lies here", he remarked to the friend. Twice during the six days of evidence an intervention by MacBride led to angry confrontations between himself and Murnaghan. Each time MacBride sought permission to inspect the New Inn police barrack records; each time Murnaghan objected and each time Troy, while showing that his sympathies were with MacBride, declined to make the order MacBride sought. By now all concerned knew that Gleeson's solicitor John Timoney had acquired another client, Thomas Reid (who had complained about his treatment in the police station) and, of course, the entries in the barracks records would probably have been of assistance to any case Timoney might make for him.

Before trying to assess the strength of the case made against Gleeson so far, the question arises as to whether or not MacBride was right not to cross-examine any of the State witnesses. Cross-examination of Guards or doctors might, after all, have yielded information that could have been useful in defending Gleeson at the subsequent jury trial. However, it appears that at the time cross-examination at the depositions stage was the exception rather than the rule. Yet, as the years passed MacBride seems to have had doubts on this score. Twice in the early 1970s, when interviewed about his career, he returned to the Gleeson case in terms suggesting that he was still troubled by it. Not long before his death, he admitted when discussing the case with people in Co. Tipperary that the case should never have got beyond the District Court. He implied that, had he cross-examined, he would have exposed serious flaws in the prosecution case.

For flaws there undoubtedly were in the case made against Gleeson in Clonmel. Given the circumstances of Moll Carthy's death, circumstantial evidence was the best the State could produce, and if satisfactory is sufficient in such a case. But how wide can the gap be between direct and circumstantial evidence to warrant a District Justice sending an accused person for trial? The case against Gleeson was that Moll Carthy died around the time Thomas Hennessy heard two shots on the evening of 20 November, when he was some three-quarters of a mile from the scene. None of the evidence placed Gleeson anywhere near where the body was found at the time Hennessy said he heard the shots. Moreover, he was the only person in the whole of New Inn to hear them. The State's own medical evidence cast doubt on whether the body could have lain at that spot all night. If it did, why when Patrick went out near midnight searching for his mother did the family dog not sense his presence? The technical evidence fell far short of suggesting the probability that the gun produced had killed Moll Carthy, or even that it had been fired at all on 20 November. Neither fingerprint evidence nor any other technical evidence was produced that in any way connected Gleeson with the shots that Hennessy said he had heard.

To establish a motive on Gleeson's part, evidence of an improper relationship with Moll Carthy was required. If such a relationship existed, the Guards should have had no difficulty in locating reliable evidence of it. Yet they seem to have been forced to rely solely on the evidence of Moll's three children, one of whom was not yet into his teens, and another only barely out of them – evidence, moreover, that seems to have suggested merely the normal acquaintance one would have expected from next-door neighbours, whose paths literally crossed every day. If one excludes the quarrel in McCarthy's yard between Gleeson and the two boys, one has to infer from the evidence of the three children little more than the possibility of some improper relationship between Gleeson and the dead woman. As to the quarrel in the yard, it was sworn to, not by the two boys who took part in it, but by a spectator, Supt. Mahony. Moreover, he had been accompanied to the scene by at least one other Guard who was never identified, let alone produced in court.

Chapter 4

'A crafty, cold-blooded murder'

The trial of Harry Gleeson began on the morning of Monday 17 February, 1941 in Dublin in the historic Green Street courthouse, where the Central Criminal Court sits. The twelve jurymen – women rarely sat on juries in that pre-feminist era – chosen by lot to decide Gleeson's guilt or innocence were:-

Michael Campbell, restaurant proprietor, 90 Talbot St. (foreman);
Christopher Lambe, contractor, 15 Newgrove Ave., Sandymount;
Louis Sandross, clerk, 147 Clonliffe Rd., Drumcondra;
Joseph Fahy, draper's assistant, 55 Connaught St., Phibsboro;
Joseph Halliday, accountant, 3 Belmont Gardens, Donnybrook;
Henry Ivers, engineer, 271 Harold's Cross Rd., Terenure;
Thomas Verling, grocer, 9 Conquer Hill Rd., Clontarf;
Joseph Parker, clerk, 109 South Circular Rd., Kilmainham;
George Sargeant, insurance official, 13 Swords Rd., Whitehall;
Andrew Wall, taxi owner, 18 Upper St. Columba's Rd., Glasnevin;
Andrew Thompson, auctioneer, 44 George's St., Dun Laoghaire;
Thomas Markey, clerk, 6 Temple Hill, Blackrock.

As a glance at this list suggests, Harry Gleeson's fate – indeed his very life – was now in the hands of a dozen Dublin middle-class, business or professional men. A majority of the twelve was probably self-employed, with the remaining five describing themselves as clerks (3), an insurance official and a draper's assistant. It is most unlikely that any of the twelve belonged to the same social background as Gleeson, or even knew much about his way of life. The presiding judge, on whose handling of the trial much also depended, was Mr. Justice Martin Maguire. A leading State prosecutor for most of the 1930s, he had only been appointed a judge a year earlier. Leading for the prosecution was Joseph A. McCarthy SC, another experienced prosecutor and later also a judge. His junior counsel was George Murnaghan, destined for promotion to the bench too, and the last Irish judge to pass a sentence of death that was actually carried out.

Leading the inexperienced Sean MacBride for the defence was James

Nolan-Whelan SC, then in his late fifties. A colourful and eccentric personality, he had been practising for almost forty years, but had only become a senior counsel in 1937. Now past his prime and dogged by ill-health, he specialised in criminal work. A professional footballer in his student days, Whelan was a lifelong follower of the turf and was reputed to have gone through several inheritances through his gambling. He was not, however, Gleeson's solicitor's first choice to defend Harry Gleeson. Timoney had first approached Patrick Lynch, King's Counsel, who had been suggested by Gleeson's family. A native of Clare, Lynch had the dubious distinction of being the defeated candidate in the 1917 Clare bye-election won by the young Eamonn de Valera. Later he became a convert to republicanism and was rewarded by being appointed Attorney General by the Fianna Fail government in 1936, a post he held until 1940. Since he had become a barrister 53 years earlier in 1888, Lynch by 1940 was into his seventies and had not practised for some years.

At the start of the trial, which was to take ten full days (from 17 to 27 February) Joseph A. McCarthy SC made a surprising move. He asked the judge to amend the charge to read "on or about the 20th or 21st November", that is, either on the Wednesday, when Moll Carthy was last seen alive by her family, or on the Thursday, when her body was found. Nolan-Whelan consented, remarking that Gleeson was most anxious to have the facts fully investigated. But, he asked, did this mean that the prosecution case for the 20th November was insupportable? Over half-a-century later this remains one of the unanswered questions in the case. It was then Nolan-Whelan's turn to make an unusual application. He asked the judge to direct the court stenographer to record the opening address to the jury for the State. Possibly he hoped that if McCarthy knew his speech was being recorded he might be less emotional. Maguire turned down his request.

For the State Joseph A. McCarthy SC now made his opening speech for the prosecution, one of the most important stages in the trial. In it he would outline the State case against Gleeson, giving the jury a summary of the evidence the prosecution would offer in order to prove the charge. At this early stage in the trial the State has to put all its cards face-up on the table. Moreover, it has to satisfy the jury of Gleeson's guilt beyond a reasonable doubt. In the District Court it had merely to establish a prima facie case against him – that is, to present sufficient evidence to persuade the District Justice that Gleeson had a case to answer and should be sent for trial by jury. McCarthy's speech lasted over three hours. It began on a high emotional note. Recalling the morning the body was found and describing the brutal injuries to it, he told of Gleeson's arrival at the local police station – "the first intimation the...authorities got of a murder that was as crafty, cold-blooded and as black-hearted as the mind of man could conceive..." Gleeson's denial that he knew either the woman or the dog was, McCarthy said, "one of the many steps taken by the accused to conceal his association with the act he had done..." The prosecution would show that "the murder was committed by...some person who knew her...whose presence on Caesar's land would not be a surprise...someone who had knowledge of where Mary McCarthy would...go and had easy access and means of escape". That person, McCarthy said, [who] had "cunningly contrived an ambush, trapped and shot her and...endeavoured to mutilate her beyond recognition..was in the dock".

Caesar, McCarthy said, owned a licensed shot-gun and bought 25 cartridges in Cashel in early October. This gun was used by Gleeson. The dead woman lived "in a humble little cottage on a little plot of ground" and was "the unfortunate mother of seven illegitimate children". She got potatoes by stealth, one of those who gave her them being Gleeson. When they heard the evidence, they would agree that the association between her and the accused was an immoral one. On Wednesday afternoon 20 November she was at home and Gleeson was on "his farm". Around 6.30, when it was dusk and she had given the children a meal she left, followed by "her little black dog" and watched by her son Michael. At about the same time Gleeson was out of the Caesar home, and between 6.30 and 7.00 p.m. a neighbour Thomas Hennessy heard two shots. "Those were the shots that killed Mary McCarthy". Back at Caesar's Gleeson, although he usually visited a neighbour on Wednesdays, stayed in, retiring "earlier than...on any previous occasion", although there were visitors in the house.

McCarthy then summarised the events of that night and the following morning as seen by the two McCarthy boys. He also previewed the evidence to be given by the State Pathologist as to the probable time of death. The finding on Caesar's premises of a sack belonging to the dead woman, and an experiment carried out with her son Michael, were then described. The State case, McCarthy said, was that this sack had been given by Moll to Gleeson on Tuesday, when the Wednesday evening meeting between them, at which she was killed, was arranged. Needless to say, McCarthy's speech was heavily biased against Gleeson and contained selective details intended to poison the jurymen's minds against him. There was an underlying assumption that he was guilty, and that only he could have committed the murder. His denial of recognition of either the body or the dog, which at that stage (before any evidence had been given) must have seemed incredible, had given the picture of a cunning deceitful person. They were intended, McCarthy said, "to divert attention from his own responsibility, to endeavour to convey to the Guards his willingness to assist and to put himself forward as a person whose conduct was consistent with innocence..."

As in the District Court, almost fifty witnesses gave evidence in the Central Criminal Court. In most cases the evidence was similar to that given in the lower court. However, some witnesses did change their evidence and occasionally the differences, though slight, were significant. Two factors influenced much of the evidence before the jury. The first was the heavier responsibility now on the prosecution – to prove the charge beyond reasonable doubt, and not merely to make an answerable case, as was sufficient in the District Court. But this was not all. An important feature of the jury that was missing in the first hearing was the more detailed evidence, even of the minor witnesses. Moreover, since no cross-examination took place in the lower court, a distinct anti-Gleeson bias had resulted there. In addition, Gleeson himself did not give any evidence there, so that, as District Justice Troy commented at the end, only one side of the story came out, and that was the one tending to incriminate Gleeson. In Green St. all this was changed. First, all the major State witnesses gave fuller versions of their evidence. Then every State witness was cross-examined before the jury by Gleeson's lawyers, and thus tested on both his facts and his credibility. Finally, after the case was complete the defence was able to put Gleeson himself in the box, and called its own professional witnesses to support his defence.

Again, as in the lower court, the State relied on the testimony of a small number of major witnesses to prove the charge against Gleeson. This core group of about six comprised Michael McCarthy, Supt. Mahony, Dr. McGrath, Supt. Stapleton, Tommy Reid and Guard Quinlan. In this account of the trial, rather than repeat their evidence, an attempt will be made to assess their impact on the jury and to point to what appear to be significant differences from the account each gave in the District Court. The evidence of Michael McCarthy, the youngest of the three children, took most of Day 2 of the ten-day hearing. Comparison with his evidence in Clonmel reveals four factual differences; if none alone was important, the cumulative effect is significant. He now said he had been at school on the Wednesday; he omitted to state what time his mother left home that afternoon; he did not say that his mother had told him the identity of the father of the last child; he omitted to mention the curious scarcity of potatoes at home on Tuesday and Wednesday.

These differences assume some importance in the light of accusations later made by Gleeson's lawyers that Michael's story had been "engineered", apparently meaning that he had been coached by the Guards. His admission to having been at school on Wednesday denied the defence the chance to compare his story with his sister's. His failure to say what time his mother left plugged another obvious gap in his evidence. By not saying that she told him who Peggy's father was, he probably denied the defence the chance to call Miss Cooney to give rebutting evidence.

40

And the failure to repeat the story of the scarce potatoes suggested that the State felt that this looked like a contrived link between his mother and Gleeson. Under cross-examination by Nolan-Whelan, Michael added to the mystery of Sergt. Daly's visit to his home by admitting that he was not sure if it had been on Tuesday or Wednesday. Neither Whelan nor the judge could find out from him if his mother had used the pump in the field since the death of his sister in May; but he did admit that he never saw Gleeson give potatoes to his mother. Once again, as in the District Court, he made no mention of the confrontation in the yard between himself his brother and Gleeson.

As to the probable impact Michael made on the jury, not even the impersonal nature of the transcript can conceal the unsatisfactory nature of his evidence. Frequently he hesitated before answering, even when helped by the judge or State counsel. A couple of times the judge lost patience with the boy. On other occasions Michael failed to answer at all, or just indicated that he did not know the answer, as if unsure about what answer he was expected to give. He admitted that he did not know the age of his younger brother Connie, that he could not count beyond ten, that he was unable to read a clock. He said his mother sometimes drew water from a farm at least a mile from her house belonging to a family named Leamy; to this day this farm still has no water supply of its own. Curiously, Michael called his neighbour Condon, from whom they got their daily milk supply, Tom rather than Jim. Sean MacBride noted in his case notebook about Michael McCarthy that he was "diminutive in size and timid-looking". The official record of the trial is peppered with examples of the difficulty both Nolan-Whelan and the judge had in getting the boy to answer important questions. The following extract may give a flavour of the exchanges:-

800. THE JUDGE:	Did you ever draw water from the well after the child died? Yes, sir.
801. THE JUDGE:	Did you ever draw water from this pump of Caesar's after the child died in May last – did you ever take water from Caesar's pump after? No answer.
802. THE JUDGE:	Could you say whether or not you took water from Caesar's pump after the little child died in May last? I don't know.
803. THE JUDGE:	Did your mother take it – did she ever go to the pump after the little child died in May last? I think she did sir, but I did not see her. I am not rightly sure.

804.MR. NOLAN-WHELAN:	You say you got water from Halpin's pump that came down stream in the Summer: Yes.
805.	What was this your Mammy said – "She would put him up to law to pay for the child". Are you sure that did not take place before the burial of the baby in May? No answer.
806.THE JUDGE:	Might that have taken place before the death of Peggie? (No answer).
807.MR.NOLAN-WHELAN:	Do you know for certain if that conversation took place before or after the death of Peggie? I don't know.
808.	Now, tell my Lord and the jury how you come to fix the time that you told my friend, the month of Peggie's funeral. How did you come to tell that? (No answer).
809.THE JUDGE:	How did you come to say that? Listen Michael, how did you come to say that conversation took place the month after the funeral. Is it correct? Yes.
810.	Do you say now it was the month after the funeral? Yes.
811.	Do you remember telling my Lord and the jury that you did not remember whether it was before or after the birth, but you now say it was a month after the funeral. How long did Peggie live? Three weeks.
812.	Are you certain – would you not say it was before the funeral? No.
813	How do you come to remember that? (No answer).

Only minutes earlier the following exchange (if that be the appropriate term) had taken place.

739.	Do you remember your mother going to that pump on many occasions after May, that is after the baby was born? (No answer).
740. THE JUDGE:	Can you say, Michael? No sir.
741. MR. NOLAN-WHELAN:	Can you not remember the baby being

	born – can you not tell my Lord and the jury if yourself and your mother drew water from Caesar's pump in the field after the burial of the baby? (No answer).
742. THE JUDGE:	You remember the last Summer? Yes sir.
743. THE JUDGE:	Now, Michael, no one is trying to confuse you or to get you to say anything that is wrong, but did you see your mother draw any water from the pump in Caesar's field last Summer? Where did you get the water from that was used in the house during the summer? Did you ever get any water last Summer yourself? Yes.
744. THE JUDGE:	Where did you get it? (No answer).
745. THE JUDGE:	Oh, go on. You have said that you got water last Summer and you must know where you got it. Where did you get it? (No answer).
746. MR. NOLAN-WHELAN:	You told this gentleman, Mr. Murnaghan, that your mother used go to the pump, and would she use the big churn? When mother went I was generally with her.
747.	Your mother used to go to the pump and you were with her; was that before or after the last baby was born? No answer.

When on Day 6 Supt. Mahony took the stand he retold, in substantially the same terms as he had in the lower court, his account of the confrontation in the yard between Gleeson and the two boys. This time he read from notes, and as he began to do so Nolan-Whelan objected. Patrick had by now also given evidence, and Whelan pointed out that neither boy had told the jury of this scene. The State was now, in effect, trying to give secondary evidence – repairing the omission by either boy to tell of the scene. A prolonged wrangle followed between judge and defence counsel. Eventually Mr. Justice Maguire ruled in favour of admitting the conversation, but only as evidence of what was said in Gleeson's presence rather than of facts stated by either boy. Nolan-Whelan pointed out that Gleeson had denied both the allegation of a planned meeting with Moll and that of paternity. Later that day at the end of the State case Nolan-Whelan pressed Maguire for a clear ruling, and the judge, while not altering his earlier decision, confirmed it in terms more favourable to the defence, as if he had since had some doubt about it – a point later taken up in the appeal court.

Probably more than any other witness in the trial, the evidence of Supt. Mahony, which was crucial to the prosecution case, showed the value of cross-examination. Concentrating on the notes the judge allowed Mahony to consult, Gleeson's lawyer suggested that he had omitted some exchanges between himself and Gleeson. Among these were a remark that Gleeson was a liar and would hang, and another that a blood-test (never carried out) would prove he was the father of the last child. Nolan-Whelan suggested to Mahony that his notes had not been made at the time; in such a case only contemporaneous notes are permissible. Bit by bit by patient probing Whelan elicited damaging admissions. Mahony admitted that the exchange between the boys and Gleeson had gone some distance before he began to make notes of it. (According to local tradition, emanating indirectly from the police, a Guard concealed in the Carthy cottage or outhouse to record the conversation was unable to hear it). Moreover, Mahony's notes were so illegible or makeshift that when he returned to his station he either filled them out or commenced them again in another notebook. Pressed to say where the original notes were, he admitted he had lost them because he had to use the notebook concerned for another purpose. He had, he eventually conceded, torn out some of the original pages, and the notes he was now using in court were reconstructed ones. When Nolan-Whelan again suggested that they did not record the whole of the exchange, the judge, in what looks like a "rescue operation", intervened and Whelan gave up.

Later Nolan-Whelan asked the Supt. about a visit he had paid to Limerick jail before Gleeson was transferred to Mountjoy jail in Dublin. Initially Gleeson was lodged in a cell with two other criminal suspects, apparently in the hope that while talking to them he would make incriminating admissions. Long after the trial was over Mahony admitted to Gleeson's solicitor that the Attorney General had ruled against the use of such evidence. However, the facts had now to be dragged from Mahony. He admitted that he had been in the prison before Christmas and had interviewed Gleeson's two cell-mates in the governor's office – "to find out if...Gleeson might have said something to them". Under further pressure he agreed that after his visit Gleeson had asked for (and got) a separate cell. Asked about Gleeson's statement of 25 November, the Supt. admitted that he had persuaded Gleeson to make it by telling him that he had "some questions" to ask him, in the context of the much shorter earlier statement. As this second statement was to take thirteen hours, Nolan-Whelan suggested that Mahony had deceived Gleeson. Predictably, Mahony disagreed.

The State Pathologist, Dr. John McGrath, who spent most of Day 5 in the box, should have been as important a witness for the State as Supt. Mahony. One of the leaders of his profession and also a university professor, he was for many years a familiar and respected figure at criminal trials. Dr. McGrath had already told his story twice, at the inquest and in the District Court. Because of his experience and expertise and not least his patent fairmindedness, his evidence and his opinions were frequently accepted without question by judges and jurors. In the Gleeson case, however, Dr. McGrath had an unusually rough passage, and when he left the stand State counsel may have wondered about his impact on the jury. He was subjected to a gruelling cross-examination by Sean MacBride, who had probably been briefed by his own medical expert, soon to take the stand for the defence. MacBride in fact asked Dr. McGrath over 200 questions, compared to 150 for the State. MacBride's probing queries seem to have irked the judge, unaccustomed perhaps to hearing McGrath's views challenged. He frequently intervened (as indeed he did with several other major witnesses) in what to a reader of the transcript over fifty years later seems an unjudicial manner. Still, as in the case of Supt. Mahony, it is likely that any imperfections in the State Pathologist's evidence were overlooked by the jury when it later retired to reach its verdict.

As usual, Dr. McGrath was scrupulously fair. He confirmed Dr. O'Connor's evidence on two matters – about the dead woman's legs being crossed and (in reply to a query from the bench) about there being "something wrong in the way the...clothes were not disarranged". He believed the body had been moved after she was shot. Also, the grass and stones under the body "looked and felt dry", and he himself had found two cartridges under the body when it was moved. Her coat had been re-buttoned after the shots and her head moved. Asked about the probable date and time of death, Dr. McGrath said that from an analysis of the stomach and intestines she had a meal of tea and bread, and had died within two to five hours after her last meal. On the basis of rigor mortis, he believed death had taken place fifteen hours before his examination; this would have placed the time of death after Gleeson had found the body. Based on the body temperature, Dr. McGrath said the time of death was 24 to 48 hours before his examination, making it any time from one o'clock on Thursday afternoon (again several hours after the body was found) back to one o'clock on Wednesday afternoon, when Moll Carthy was still alive.

Near the end of his direct evidence Dr. McGrath was asked about his analysis of Gleeson's clothes. He said he had found semen stains on the front of a shirt, and more on the trousers. In his cross-examination Sean MacBride dealt first with these stains. Dr. McGrath accepted that such stains were normal on male clothing that had been worn for a long time, and agreed that they could have been there for months. Regarding the body temperature, MacBride got the witness to agree that if Moll Carthy had died around 6.30 p.m. on Wednesday, as the State had claimed, it was 44 hours after death when he took the temperature. He then got agreement from Dr. McGrath, that when he carried out his examination around lunchtime on the Friday, the woman had been dead for at least fifteen hours. This, of course, supported the theory being advanced by the defence that she had been murdered on the Thursday morning. Turning next to temperature as a factor in fixing the time of death, MacBride got Dr. McGrath to agree that if Dr. O'Connor's finding of 96 degrees Fahrenheit at 11.30 on Thursday morning was correct (something the State did not challenge), this could not be squared with death having occurred around 6.30 the previous evening. It was, said the pathologist, frankly "inexplicable". He even went further. If one excluded the dog as a factor in determining the heat of the body (a line the State had not pursued), the time of death could have been much closer – perhaps even an hour or two – to the time of Dr. O'Connor's examination before midday on Thursday.

Several times during Dr. McGrath's evidence Mr. Justice Maguire intervened, as if trying to elicit facts favourable to the prosecution. With such a formidable and frank expert as Dr. McGrath, he did not always succeed. When asked if there had been any blood around the site where the body lay, Dr. McGrath played down the amount he had found. When asked about the view through the fence, Nolan-Whelan strenuously objected because, he pointed out, this was a medical and not an engineering witness. The judge allowed the question; but Dr. McGrath hedged noticeably and when during cross-examination MacBride returned to this topic Dr. McGrath added several new qualifications that made his evidence on the point almost valueless. In the end, however, the judge scored a major victory. Just as Dr. McGrath was about to leave the box, he asked a final question. "From your...post-mortem examination...was there anything inconsistent with...this woman having been shot between 6.30 and 7.00 on Wednesday 20th November?" Gleeson's lawyers must have been horrified to hear a single "No" in reply, since it was totally at variance with the concessions MacBride's patient questioning had wrung from this vital witness. It was, of course, a trick question from an experienced prosecuting lawyer. The significance of the phrase "from your...examination" was probably lost on the jury. This prevented Dr. McGrath from considering Dr. O'Connor's examination, which he had already largely accepted.

The evidence of Superintendent Daniel Stapleton, the ballistics expert from police headquarters, was an important part of the prosecution case. However, because of its technical nature, it seems unlikely that much of it was fully understood by the jury, unless any juryman was familiar with firearms. In his direct evidence Stapleton said that Moll Carthy could have been first shot by a person standing at the far side of the gap from where she was found. Describing experiments he had carried out with Caesar's gun, using cartridges handed up by Caesar, he said that two of the cartridges found in the vicinity of the body had been used recently, and could have been fired from Caesar's gun around Wednesday 20 November, the day the dead woman was last seen alive. Under prolonged cross-examination (lasting three times longer than his direct testimony) by MacBride, Stapleton modified some of his earlier conclusions. He eventually conceded that the two cartridges he had said could have been used around 20 November could in fact have been used any time back to 14 November. When challenged about the view of the body that Gleeson would have had on the Thursday morning through the fence, Stapleton conceded that one had to climb partly up on to the fence in order to see the whole of the body.

Off all the witnesses from the New Inn locality called by the prosecution, none was more important that Tommy Reid. As the person who, even more than the two Caesars, spent most of the day in Gleeson's company, he was in a position to supply vital information to the Guards on such matters as Gleeson's daily routine and, more importantly, his movements in the days and hours leading up to his fateful walk into New Inn police station on Thursday 21 November. However, the Guards, by their (apparently literally) ham-fisted treatment of Reid, appear to have under-estimated both the dominating influence of Mrs. Caesar and Reid's loyalty to Gleeson. By seemingly concentrating their efforts, in their marathon session in the station on 25 November with Reid, on extracting information that would confirm their theory of a Thursday morning murder by Gleeson, they deprived themselves of a chance to question Reid about the comings and goings of Gleeson on the Tuesday and Wednesday.

As a result, although the State had no option but to call Reid, they ran the risk that he might do their case more harm than good. As he was taken meticulously through the events at Marlhill on both the Wednesday (the day the Caesars went to town) and the Thursday (the day the body was found), it became clear that only direct questions (not permissible, as Reid was a State witness) would prise much more out of Reid than the little he had told the District Court. On several occasions, his reluctance to give away anything he felt might damage Gleeson became obvious. When he got the chance to do so, he accused the Guards of having beaten him in the station, showing where his sympathies lay, and also angering the judge. From Maguire's critical comments during Reid's evidence it is clear that he created an unfavourable impression on the judge, who seems to have regarded him as an unreliable witness for the State. Reid's reluctance at times to give full answers, and his occasionally casual manner, led Maguire on several occasions to warn him to pay attention, to give a straight answer, and once even to remind him he was on oath. Given that in so many ways the jury seem to have taken a lead from the bench, it is likely that Reid was more useful to the State case than he himself would have wished.

If, as suggested above, Mr. Justice Maguire showed bias during the evidence of Supt. Mahony and Dr. McGrath, it became even more obvious during the evidence of the police mapping expert, Guard William Quinlan. In a case such as Gleeson's, involving complicated references to features of the terrain unfamiliar to both judge and jury, proper and accurate maps were essential. In this case the State also had a set of twelve police photographs prepared and handed in as evidence. Like Supt. Stapleton and Dr. McGrath, Quinlan was an experienced witness well known to judges and lawyers, including Maguire. In a two-hour cross-examination MacBride showed up some deficiencies and omissions in Quinlan's direct evidence. He had said that the gap in the fence through which Gleeson saw the body was nine feet wide; now he reduced it to five-and-a-half feet, thus narrowing Gleeson's field of vision. He admitted that his map incorrectly placed the body on the wrong side of the gap; it was in fact some nine or ten feet from where he marked it. He had also placed the body 27 feet from the junction of two fields; he now reduced this to thirteen feet. His cross-examination was punctuated by interjections from the bench. "This witness is invariably clear in his evidence, but he is a little confused now", Maguire once improperly commented; on another occasion he lost patience with both Quinlan and MacBride.

The last of the core witnesses for the State was Michael Leamy, the employee in the Cashel hardware store whose function was merely to prove the purchase of cartridges by Caesar some weeks before the murder. Leamy said that on 3 October 1940 John Caesar had bought a box of 25 Eley Grand Prix cartridges. He produced a copy of the receipt he had given Caesar, and said Caesar's previous purchase had been in June 1940. Although pressed by State counsel, he could not remember what shot-number Caesar had bought; "it was usually No. 4 or No. 5". As it was customary at this stage to hand in the firearms register, with the sale recorded in it, the judge intervened and was told by Joseph A. McCarthy SC that Leamy had not brought the register to court with him. Maguire directed him to bring it next day; McCarthy remarked; "The register won't show it [meaning the shot number]; it has been examined". Cross-examined by Nolan-Whelan, Leamy admitted there was a register; again McCarthy said it had been sent for, and Leamy left the box. In fact the register was never produced, for the very good reason (as doubtless McCarthy, who had seen it, knew well) that its contents would have embarrassed the prosecution. As it happens, unlike some of the other official records relating to Gleeson's trial, the register has survived. It shows that on 3 October 1940 there were only two sales, but neither of them to Caesar. Not only that, but for the June purchase by Caesar the register has clearly been tampered with and details of Caesar's purchase (if he ever made one that month at all) entered above another transaction, the record of which has been struck out.

As in the District Court, the four New Inn Guards again all gave evidence in Green St., dealing mostly with the morning Gleeson found the body. Although their evidence followed largely the lines of their earlier testimony, under cross-examination disagreements among all four were revealed, which were naturally pounced on by Gleeson's lawyers to try to discredit the police evidence as a whole. In hindsight, one wonders if this severe questioning impressed the jury. It certainly did not commend itself to the judge, who at least twice suggested to Nolan-Whelan that his "grilling" of a Guard was pointless or excessive. The most important of the four Guards was, of course, Sergt. Daly, a central figure in the whole investigation. His gruff manner and unco-operative demeanour come through even from the transcript. He gave the impression of a man constantly on his guard, even from the State lawyers. He appears to have been a domineering, even bullying personality, accustomed to getting his own way, economical with the truth and suspicious of lawyers. Several times, when pressed to amend his account of a conversation, he said bluntly: "I only heard what I said; that is my answer". In disagreeing with his own colleagues from New Inn, he went close to calling them perjurers. Curiously, Gleeson's lawyers made no attempt to elicit from Daly the purpose of his visit to Moll Carthy's house the afternoon she was last seen alive. It was left to Mr. Justice Maguire to bring the case to a temporary halt and to confirm from the Sergt. that he had actually spoken to her that day; Nolan-Whelan, then on his feet, did not pursue the matter. It may be that, having heard Guard Ruth's explanation of his Monday visit (that he had gone to collect a school attendance fine), Nolan-Whelan assumed Daly was on the same mission. Even a moment's reflection, however, should have made him realise that Ruth's sergeant would hardly have gone out 48 hours later for the same reason.

After the two superintendents, the most senior police officer to give evidence was Inspector Thomas O'Reilly of Thurles station, whose direct testimony largely repeated what he had told the District Justice. He

Date of Transaction	Description and number of Firearms sold or hired, specifying maker's name and number. If only hired state so.	Description and quantity of Ammunition sold.	Name and Address of person to whom sold or hired.	If sale or hiring to person other than Registered Dealer number of Firearm Certificate held by the person to whom sold or hired.

Copy of Firearms Register showing change of entry and insertion of Caesar's name.

described the circumstances of taking the two statements from Gleeson and told of tests he had carried out – timing routes through Caesar's fields, calculating the chances of Thomas Hennessy having heard the two shots on Wednesday evening, checking the views at the spot where the body was found, and so on. Under cross-examination, however, O'Reilly gave some new evidence. The second statement took from 12.10 p.m. on 25 November to 10.00 a.m. on 26 November to complete. As if realising that the jury now knew that Gleeson had been kept up all night, the judge here interrupted testily to remind Nolan-Whelan that the officer had explained that the thirteen hours had included several intervals, three meals and rests for smoking. Nolan-Whelan then drew from O'Reilly the admission that most of these adjournments were for the purpose of going outside the house, where Gleeson had to explain matters in his statements.

Amongst the minor witnesses who gave different evidence in the jury trial from their testimony in the District Court were three whose revised stories to some degree benefited Gleeson. James Condon said it was 6.30 p.m. when he left Carthy's on Wednesday with his goat, thus placing Moll still at home five minutes into the period when the State alleged she was killed. His wife said that when that same evening Michael McCarthy cycled over for the milk he stayed until 6.30, something that fits in with his statement of last seeing his mother alive "around 7 or 8 o'clock". Frank Lenehan, the local man who saw Michael out of doors early on Thursday morning, said he was out cycling on Wednesday afternoon when Hennessy heard two shots; but Lenehan heard none. When Supt. Mahony left the box on Day 6, the prosecution case closed. Before opening the defence case Nolan-Whelan returned to the accusations made against Gleeson by the two boys in the yard. He asked the judge for a formal ruling on whether or not they would be allowed in as evidence, and once again reminded Maguire that Gleeson had denied them. Maguire replied: "I am ruling that they are merely allegations that are denied...I will...explain to the jury that they are merely allegations...as distinct from proof...I will keep you right".

A portion of the two pages of the roll-book of Knockgraffon national school for October to December 1940. Michael McCarthy, pupil No. 407, had been removed for non-attendance before October, but was restored (as pupil No. 407 again) from October, and then finally removed from December after his mother's murder. The entry in the roll for the week ending Saturday, 23 November (fifth box from the right) at No. 7, his number in the roll, clearly shows that, despite his evidence to the contrary, he attended school on Monday, Tuesday and Wednesday (November 18, 19 and 20), but was absent (because of his mother's death) on Thursday and Friday (November 21 and 22), never returning thereafter – hence the stroke through his name. The diagonal stroke (\) indicates attendance and the device ⊙ indicates absence.

Chapter 5

Gleeson's defence

At 11.20 a.m. on Day 7 Sean MacBride began the opening speech for the defence. He spoke for over four hours. Very little of the prosecution's original case now remained, he suggested. If, for example, the facts before the jury suggested that Mary McCarthy was not killed where she was found, they could not convict Gleeson. The motive for the murder advanced by the State depended on three facts – that he was the father of the last child, that there had been an immoral relationship and that she had been blackmailing him. The only evidence for paternity was the conversation Michael McCarthy had heard when his mother threatened law to Gleeson. Regarding the confrontation in the yard between the two boys and Gleeson, he suggested that this whole scene had been engineered by the Guards, who had primed the boys for the occasion. Why did neither boy describe the event when on oath? Regarding the opportunity and the means to commit the crime, MacBride said that nearly everybody in the area had the same opportunity. As to the means, the Guards admitted that shot-guns of the same type were owned by all the farmers in New Inn.

Dealing with Dr. McGrath's evidence, MacBride reminded the jury of the concessions the pathologist had made. He confirmed that hardly any blood was found at or near the scene. The odd position of the clothes, MacBride suggested, meant that she had been carried by the arms; if this was so, she had been shot before she was brought to where she had been found. The night had been wet, yet her clothes were dry; Dr. McGrath had even found mud on the back of her coat, although the ground underneath was dry. Analysing the evidence about the body temperature, MacBride said that if Mary McCarthy died on Wednesday Gleeson was not her killer. Both doctors called by the State found the body temperature inexplicable; but this was only so if one assumed death occurred that evening. He would produce medical evidence suggesting that the temperature of 96 degrees found by Dr. O'Connor, and the lower one found the next day by Dr. McGrath, were both inconsistent with the woman having died before 6.00 a.m. on Thursday.

Regarding Reid's evidence, MacBride reminded the jury that Reid's own counsel had challenged parts of it. Having called him to give evidence against Gleeson, the State could not accept parts of his testimony as satisfactory and reject other parts because it supported Gleeson's innocence. If Reid was prepared to commit perjury, he could, MacBride said, have provided Gleeson with a complete alibi – a remarkable "shot in the dark", as will be shown later in this book. Finally MacBride outlined the evidence his engineer would give. He would tell the jury that from the top of the gap in the fence on to which Gleeson had partly climbed, he could not see the head of the body. He would also tell them that from where Michael McCarthy said he saw Gleeson cross the gap with a dog, the boy could not see the dog. He suggested that in denying that he recognised the woman or the dog, Gleeson had nothing to gain, and must have told the truth.

At 4.15 on Day 7 Harry Gleeson took the stand as the principal witness for the defence. He was to be in the box for the rest of that day and most of the next, by far the longest witness in the whole trial, answering no less than 912 questions. In his direct examination Nolan-Whelan asked only forty questions. First, he formally proved Gleeson's two statements, pointing out that both had been made without legal assistance. Gleeson said he had no lawyer until he was brought to Limerick jail after the Clonmel hearings. He agreed that the two McCarthy boys had made the allegations against him that Supt. Mahony had testified to; but he had denied them at the time, and he did so again now. He swore that Moll Carthy had never threatened to bring him to court over her last child. He had last used Caesar's gun about a week before her body was found, because the previous day he had seen a fox with a goose. Asked if he had ever been in court before, he said the only time was when he went into a public-house in Cahir to buy cigarettes after closing-time, and the technical charge had been dismissed. Finally, he told the jury he was not the father of the last Carthy child; he had never had an immoral association with the dead woman, and he had no "hand, act or part" in the murder. In effect, Nolan-Whelan had called Gleeson principally to make a formal sworn statement of his innocence, before handing him over to the State for cross-examination. Joseph A. McCarthy SC was to ask almost 840 questions, over twenty times as many as Gleeson's own counsel.

Gleeson's cross-examination began with an exchange about his alleged deafness in which the judge took a hand, showing apparent disbelief of Gleeson. McCarthy then tried to show that Gleeson had lied in saying he had not recognised the body or the dog. Gleeson explained that she had always a succession of dogs and that, as Reid worked around the yard, he would have been more familiar with them. There followed questions about visitors to Caesar's home who might cross the fields. The purpose was to show that Gleeson would know when people would be on the land; but he insisted that this happened only about half-a-dozen times a year. Next came questions about the gap in the fence and on the time he was up and around the morning the body was found. He said he had heard no shots around 8.30 that morning. McCarthy then took Gleeson through the events of that Thursday morning in detail.

281. MR. McCARTHY: You came down on this morning of the 21st of November. You had been out sometime? I was out since about a quarter past 8 o'clock.

282. Where were you from a quarter after 8 o'clock until quarter to nine o'clock? I had breakfast to take.

283. How long did that take? Ten or twelve minutes. Then I had the horses to let in.

284. Where did you go then? I let in the horses and fed them in the house. I brought them from the fields.

285. What time would that be? It would be anything from 8.30 o'clock.

286. At that time you didn't hear any shot? No.

287. After you fed the horses what did you do? I went over milking the cows, sir.

288. Where? Over the passage down the boreen.

289. Did you go down the pump field? Yes, sir.

290. How long were you with the horses? The horses would not take very long – about five minutes.

291. So at twenty five minutes to 9 o'clock you went down the lane to the pump field? Yes.

292. When you were going down the lane, I think you were three fields away at your own place from the dug-out? Yes, sir.

293. And from twenty-five minutes to 9 o'clock whilst you were out, did you hear any shot? No, sir.

294. THE JUDGE: Did you hear any shot at all that morning? No, sir.

295. MR. McCARTHY: You began in the pump field milking cows? Yes.

296. What time did you leave that? It would be shoving towards half past 9 o'clock or thereabouts.

297.THE JUDGE:	That would leave you in the pump field almost an hour? I would not know, I would be milking that time; I might be there anything about half an hour to an hour.
298.MR. McCARTHY:	Anyway you were in the pump field long before five minutes to nine o'clock. Had you a view from where you were milking the cows of Mary McCarthy's house and yard? I had, sir.
299.	Were you looking in that direction? You could not be when doing the milking of cows.
300.	Then you were not, did you look in that direction? No, sir.
301.	So that Michael McCarthy saw you from the yard there at five minutes to 9 o'clock looking in your direction and you did not see him? No, sir.
302.	How far away from where you were looking was Michael McCarthy's cottage? I suppose it would be 3 to 400 yards.
303.	So then you went back again I take it to the house? Yes, sir.
304.	And you then came down about the back of Dan Gorman's? Yes, sir.
305.	You then put your hand on the fence. Will you show us now here and you stood at this fence? Show me the Map and I will show you.
306.	No, show it here? I had a dog in my right hand and I would be going straight to the fence and I had one hand on the ditch and my foot on the step and when I looked over the ditch a dog growled at me and I gave a look and I saw the woman.
307.	You looked over the fence first? Yes
308.	And the dog growled at you? Yes.
309.	Did you make any noise? No, sir.
310.	So that you made no noise but the dog growled at you? Well, when I came to him in a hurry and he saw me he growled.
311.	But you came from the other side of Gorman's pound? Yes.

John Caesar's house, long since demolished. (Garda files)

Mary McCarthy's cottage, 1940. It is now (1993) in ruins. (Garda files)

Harry Gleeson in front of horse and cart. Note the dog under the cart.

Harry Gleeson in a 'posed' photograph in a cornfield.

Harry Gleeson, an accomplished fiddle player.

The 'field pump' from which the McCarthys drew water (on Caesar's land). (Garda files)

In this picture of a hurling team, probably taken in the New Inn area in the 1920s, Harry Gleeson is the fourth from right in the second row, with peak of cap turned sideways.

New Inn Garda station.

John J. Timoney, solicitor (1910–1961).

Seán McBride (1904-1988).

312.	And then you said you looked out. How long did you look out? When the dog growled at me I gave a look and the dog growled and I doubled back again and turned.
313.THE JUDGE:	Why did you do that? I could not go out and I having a hound with me. I looked out and seen the woman and I doubled off the ditch.
314.	Why did you go away and leave a woman lying there? I came to the conclusion that it was the best thing to do.
315.MR. McCARTHY:	When you looked out at the woman she was according to Superintendent Stapleton's evidence about 8 feet 11 inches away from your eye. Would that be about right? I cannot tell, sir.
316.	Right underneath you? Yes, underneath me mostly.
317.	And you saw the dog you said as in your statement it was lying on her chest? Yes, sir.
318.	You knew Mary McCarthy? Yes, sir.
319.	How far away was her chest from her chin? I don't understand you.
320.	Show us where you saw the dog. About here (indicating on his own chest).
321.	And you tell these twelve gentlemen of the jury that you saw the dog's head that way and you saw nothing else? I didn't, sir.
322.	How did you know that this woman was either dead or sleeping? This conclusion I came to when I seen her lying.
323.	How did you come to that conclusion? When I seen her lying down there.
324.	You thought of what you were going to do? No. The conclusion was when I came to the fence, the impression I got was that the woman was either sleeping or dead.
325.	From what? When I seen her lying there.
326.	For all you knew she might have only fallen there? It could happen.
327.	Why didn't you think of that; why did you come to the conclusion that she might be

	dead or only sleeping? Well, I didn't bother my head about it. I didn't bother seeing about her, but I doubled back from the ditch on the spot.
328.	But people, of course, used to cross you land according to yourself here, your neighbours? Yes.
329.	Did it occur that it might be one of you neighbour's wives or daughters? No, sir.
330.	Why? Well, I don't know.
331.THE JUDGE:	You didn't know, why that didn't occur to you. What did you not know? I didn't know the person when I came to the ditch.

On Day 8 Gleeson spent most of it in the box, with his very life depending on how he stood up to the continued cross-examination. For a start, McCarthy returned to the scene the morning Gleeson found the body, and criticised him for not having helped the woman lying in the field. Gleeson explained that he had to leave because of the growling dog and the fact that he had his own hound to keep under control. When McCarthy reminded him that Supt. Stapleton had no difficulty recognising the body as that of a woman, Gleeson replied that there was then no dog lying on it. McCarthy then dealt with the cartridges found near the body. He made no progress about some that had been twisted; Gleeson simply denied that this was a habit of his. The judge, who seemed to be puzzled by this evidence, took the unusual course of getting Gleeson to twist a cartridge in court; this he did quite coolly. When asked repeatedly about where the cartridges were kept, he insisted that he always got ammunition from his uncle or aunt from a stock kept in their bedroom.

Suddenly as if hoping to catch Gleeson off-guard, McCarthy switched to the dead woman's family. He began with questions about her daughter. How well did he know her? How often did he meet her? How would he greet her? What conversation would he have with her? Gleeson's answers gave the impression that he hardly knew the girl at all. He even declined, when pressed, to subscribe to the local view that she was slightly mentally retarded. McCarthy then tried to establish from Gleeson that he had had an immoral liaison with Moll. He was asked when and how often he met her in the fields, what business they would have there and what conversation took place. There was no direct accusation, rather an attempt by subtle queries to create the impression that the pair had had the opportunity to have an improper relationship. Gleeson frankly admitted that he knew the woman and could not avoid meeting her frequently, but insisted that most of their meetings arose out of the perennial problems of her straying goats and their depredations to his uncle's land. Some of the more serious allegations Gleeson denied totally, in particular the occasion when Moll was said to have told him she would make him pay for the last child.

370. Did you have sometime prior to Mary McCarthy's death any conversation with her other than the one you have told us? That is the last conversation I had.

371. Is that the one that the daughter Mary stated she saw you talking? It would be sir.

372. Was Michael about? I don't know, sir. I cannot say who was there.

373. Where was this conversation? In the field at the front of the house.

374. In your field? Yes.

375. How did she come there? She came in turning out the goats. I was turning out the goats myself.

376. Was Michael McCarthy there – did he come on the scene? I think he was there alright.

377. And did you have a few words about the goats? I told her it is a wonder she would not tie them together, and she said "begorra it is", and she and I went away.

378. Listen to what Michael said: "Sometime after the child died Mammy went to Caesars' for the goats". Would that be the occasion? It would be sir.

379. "And he heard Gleeson and she fighting". Did you have hot words about the goats? That is all I said about the goats and about spancelling them.

380. "And Mammy said she would put him up to law to pay for the last child? I never heard that sir.

381. So this little boy according to your Counsel is either being put up to say that or is inventing it himself? I did not hear her saying it sir.

382. Could you have heard her saying it, was she near enough to you? Yes, sir.

383. Am I to understand that she did not say it? She did not.

Asked about the sack taken from around one of Caesar's pumps, Gleeson insisted that he first told Supt. Mahony about this earlier on the day he made his second statement, rather than (as the prosecution claimed) that evening when Sergt. Kelly brought in the sack found in Caesar's outhouse. McCarthy then turned to the suggestion that Moll used to get potatoes furtively from Gleeson.

465.	About the occasion on which you gave her potatoes; how did you give them to her? I was over fencing at the front of her house, and she asked me for some spuds, and she gave me a bag, and I going over in the evening I brought it to her.
466.	In her own bag? Yes, in the corner of the field. I put them through the ditch. It is the only occasion I gave her spuds.
467.THE JUDGE:	What did she say to you? She asked for a handful of spuds.
468.	What did you say to her? I said, "Give me a bag and I will give you a handful".
469.MR. McCARTHY:	Where did you leave them? I threw them over the ditch.
470.	What time? I cannot tell the time, but it would be before dark and I foddering in the fields.
471.	Did she give you a bag? She did.
472.	And you gave her back the same bag?
473.THE JUDGE:	Did you bring that bag to your house? Yes, the bag was given to me for the potatoes.
474.	And did you fill it with your uncle's potatoes? Yes.
475.	And did you let your uncle or aunt know it? I don't think they knew about it.
476.	Would your uncle have been annoyed if he knew you had been giving potatoes secretly to Mary McCarthy? He would not, sir, for she got spuds sometimes before that from my aunt at the house.

After some further exchanges about the sack found in Caesar's outhouse, the judge intervened on the topic of the confrontation in the yard between Gleeson and the two boys. Despite objections from Nolan-Whelan, Maguire permitted questions on this subject, because MacBride in his opening speech had said the scene had been "engineered" by the

Guards. However, when McCarthy went too far by giving his own summary of the event, Maguire called a halt to his cross-examination – but not before Gleeson had a chance to remind the jury that he had no appointment to meet Moll on the Wednesday evening, and also to deny that he was the father of her last child.

McCarthy then asked about the Saturday night after the murder, when the neighbour William Ryan visited Caesar's and Mrs. Caesar told of Gleeson's discovery. McCarthy tried to give the impression that, because Gleeson took no part in the conversation, he was indifferent to the murder. Gleeson said he had been reading the day's newspaper and that his aunt had dominated the conversation. Asked for his opinion of the dead woman, he agreed that she was a quiet, harmless, inoffensive woman. Of Patrick and Michael he said that, although good boys, both "have told a share of lies this time". Near the end of the cross-examination he agreed that on the Wednesday he had been out of the house from 5.45 p.m. to just after 7.00 p.m., that he passed by the Dug-Out Field around 6 o'clock and that he got back to the farmyard between 6.45 and 7.00 p.m. Asked about the area where the body was found, Gleeson conceded that it was a secluded spot. Then in twenty crucial questions Maguire returned to the contentious problem of what time exactly Gleeson got home. He told the judge he reached the yard, where he spent fifteen minutes with the dogs, before 7.00 p.m. and was in for his meal by 7.00 p.m. Maguire reminded him that Reid said it was a minute after 7 when Gleeson sat down, and that in his own statement to the Guards Gleeson said he entered the house at 6.45 p.m. and that it was not yet 7 when he asked for a newspaper. He now conceded that when making these statements he did not realise the importance of times.

How well did Gleeson perform as a witness? I have found only one person still alive who sat through the whole trial; understandably, after 53 years all this person has retained are general impressions. As a result, one is totally dependent on whatever impression can be got from the official transcript. Clearly his two days in the witness-box must have been an ordeal for Gleeson. By the time he took the oath the case against him had been presented in detail for nearly a week by some 50 witnesses, many of them his neighbours and friends. He had been portrayed as a callous, clever killer who, fearing that an immoral association with a local woman with seven children (one of whom he was accused of fathering) might get to the ears of his uncle and aunt, had lured her to her death under the pretence of being kind to her. In such circumstances it would be surprising if this obscure farm manager, who had never been out of his native county in all his 38 years, does not at times come across from the record as occasionally hesitant. There were even moments when he seemed reluctant to deny, until forced to do so, some of the major allegations against him, and even to have displayed an air of casualness, almost as if he was resigned to his fate.

Three more witnesses followed for the defence. The first, Patrick Munden, a well-known Dublin engineer and architect, had prepared two maps of the area where the body was found. MacBride took him over the details of these. Munden was followed by Dr. John C. Flood, one of the most prominent medical men in Dublin, with qualifications in forensic medicine and a big practice as a gynaecologist. He first dismissed the semen stains on Gleeson's clothes, which could, he said, have been there for from four to twelve months. He also said the body could have been shot at some place other than where it was found, then carried there and shot again. This theory seems to have taken the judge by surprise; he said he could not follow Flood. This gave Flood an opportunity to explain his reasons for his theory. The real value of Dr. Flood to Gleeson's case probably lay in two major propositions, to which he stuck throughout his evidence. First, because of the temperature Dr. O'Connor recorded the morning the body was found, Flood insisted that death had occurred only a few hours earlier that morning, rather than (as the State case required) on the previous evening. Secondly, he rejected Dr. McGrath's view that the dog lying on the body affected the body temperature to any significant degree.

The last witness, Michael Barron, a friend of Gleeson, was a director of Clonmel Greyhound Company. Living about a mile from Gleeson, he confirmed that Gleeson had a hearing defect; but they had no appointment to meet on the night of Wednesday 20 November. The evidence for both sides had taken eight full days. The official transcript, which does not contain any of counsels' speeches, fills eight substantial books closely typed on foolscap-size paper, recording almost 5,800 questions and answers – an average of 725 per day. Two more books were to be required to record the judge's charge to the jury and the subsequent exchanges with the lawyers, before the jury retired to consider their verdict.

Before the judge's charge came the closing speeches for both sides, which occupied the first half of Day 9. For Gleeson, Nolan-Whelan spoke for 80 minutes, Murnaghan for somewhat less. Mr. Justice Maguire's speech lasted for the rest of that day and until 4.00 p.m. on Day 10. It will be fully analysed later in this book. Unusually for such a trial, there were two unplanned breaks, both on the first day of Maguire's charge. When (for the second time) he commented adversely on the failure of anyone from the Caesar household to give evidence, Mrs. Caesar stood up in the gallery, and in a loud voice said: "We were not called". At the judge's direction she was ejected by the Guards. One cannot but sympathise with her action. First, evidence had in fact been given by two people from her house – Reid and Gleeson himself. Secondly, like so many others from

New Inn, the two Caesars had been served with witnesses' summons by the State, so that in practice it would have been difficult for the defence to have called either of them. Moreover, the fact that the State, having forced the elderly couple to sit through the entire ten-day trial of their nephew, chose not to call them suggests that the State felt neither of the Caesars had worthwhile evidence to give. The second interruption came when a juror had a heart attack. Shaken by the event, Maguire adjourned until the next morning when a doctor told him the man had recovered. As the court rose unexpectedly on Day 9, Gleeson found himself close to a friend from Co. Tipperary, who greeted him. "Say a prayer for me, Billy", Gleeson whispered urgently.

At the end of the charge, when the jury had been sent to their room, Nolan-Whelan made a whole series of objections to Maguire's speech. He had, Whelan claimed, completely failed to put the defence submissions regarding the paternity of the last child. He had also failed to tell the jury that the scene in the farmyard between the two boys and Gleeson had not been put to either boy, and was based entirely on Supt. Mahony's account. There had been no reference at all to the defence theory that Moll Carthy died on the Thursday morning and not on the Wednesday evening. Maguire recalled the jury and spent some time making new points to them based on Nolan-Whelan's objections. At 6.30 they were back out with a guilty verdict, but with a strong recommendation to mercy. Allowing for the brief recall, they had been in for two hours and twenty minutes.

Maguire asked Gleeson if he had anything to say as to why sentence of death should not be imposed; it was not then obligatory. From the dock Gleeson appeared first not to have appreciated what the verdict was; perhaps, like so much of the evidence, he had not heard it fully. Then, using the same formula that he had twice before, he simply said: "I had neither hand, act or part in it". A Guard who had been in Clonmel courthouse told me fifty years later that he was struck by the way that, using the same firm tone of voice as in Clonmel, Gleeson had repeated precisely the same words. Maguire then pronounced the death sentence. The date of execution was fixed as 24 March 1941. After passing sentence the judge turned to Gleeson and assured him that the jury's recommendation would be passed on to the authorities. The formal order was "that on the 24th day of March, 1941, you, Henry Gleeson, be taken to the common place of execution in the prison in which you will be confined, and that you be then and there hanged by the neck until you are dead, and that your body be buried within the walls of the prison". Gleeson was then taken back to Mountjoy jail. The friend from Tipperary who had exchanged a few brief words with him the previous day returned from his lunch in a local public-house, to meet the two Caesars leaving the courthouse in tears.

Supt. Mahony climbing the ditch towards the gap from where Harry Gleeson first saw Mary McCarthy's body. Gleeson said in his evidence that this was not, as Mahony claimed, the way he [Gleeson] came towards the gap. (Garda files)

Chapter 6

Harry is hanged

Less than twenty-four hours after his client was sentenced to death, Harry Gleeson's solicitor initiated an appeal against the jury's verdict. On 28 February a notice was lodged in the Court of Criminal Appeal, which suspended, until the appeal was decided, the order for Gleeson's hanging. The main ground of appeal was summarised in its two opening lines: "the...charge to the jury was incomplete, defective, unsatisfactory and incorrect". It listed 27 specific portions of the defence case, all of which it claimed, when taken together, amounted to a failure by the judge to put the defence case adequately to the jury. As a result, the notice of appeal claimed, his charge to the jury was "unbalanced [because] it gave undue preponderance to...the case made by the prosecution and omitted...and minimised the evidence favourable to, and the case made by, the defence". The hearing of Gleeson's appeal was fixed for 31 March, leaving his three lawyers barely a month to prepare their case.

Meanwhile, back in New Inn, as the local community tried to come to terms with the possibility that one of their neighbours would mount the scaffold in Mountjoy jail in a few weeks, events suddenly took a new turn only ten days before the opening of Gleeson's appeal. Memories were being jogged and a few consciences being disturbed. On Thursday 21 March, 1941 Thomas Gleeson, a nephew of Harry, arrived in the office of Gleeson's solicitor in Tipperary town, twelve miles from New Inn. He handed Timoney a note from the Caesars which contained this message: "There is a man in the village...a tailor, Jos. Moloney, who states he heard two shots on the morning of the death of Mary McCarthy. He told the P.P., who told him to tell the Guards, but he did not do so. The public know this". That evening Timoney phoned Sean MacBride and the following morning went by taxi to New Inn, where Moloney confirmed the contents of the note. He said another man named Coman also heard the shots. He also told Timoney that a man named Fitzgerald or Fitzpatrick had fired two shots at a cat in the locality the previous evening, and that he (Moloney) had reported this to Guard Scully. Scully later told him that Sergt. Daly had interviewed the man who had fired the shots, but this man insisted he fired only once. Moloney continued to insist that two shots had been fired on the Wednesday evening, and said a man named Gorman would say who fired them.

Timoney tracked down Coman and Gorman. Learning from Gorman that the man who had fired the shots was John Fitzgerald, Timoney visited him; Fitzgerald insisted he fired only one shot. Realising the importance of this new information, which if true supported the theory that Moll Carthy had died on the morning she was found, Timoney held a conference with his two barristers in Dublin on Monday 24 March. The next day he again hired a taxi and went to New Inn. There he interviewed six men, taking a statement from each about the shots fired on Wednesday and Thursday. All six signed their statements except Fr. O'Malley. All six statements were then attached to an application to the appeal court for further witnesses, so that when the hearing began on 31 March the court would have copies of the statements before it with the transcript of the trial.

As his statement is the basis of the other five, Joseph Moloney's is the longest. He told Timoney he was a tailor and resided at Lough Kent East, New Inn. In June 1940 a son of his, also a tailor and employed in Rockwell College, joined the army; since then Joseph had helped out occasionally in the college. On the morning of Thursday 21 November, the day the body was found, he left home on foot for Rockwell around 9.10; he remembered the Clonmel bus passing his home as he breakfasted. He went through New Inn village towards Cashel on the main Dublin-Cork road. As he reached the cross-roads in the village he saw the parish priest Fr. O'Malley leave his home a short distance away on his way to say the 9.30 Mass. Moloney had got abreast of a derelict house "a few hundred yards from the cross-roads" when he heard two shots in quick succession. In his original oral statement to Timoney (like everything else, meticulously recorded by Timoney) Moloney had said he once lived in this house, and as he walked along he was "kind of day-dreaming" when the shots came. They were from a double-barrelled gun. He had owned one many years before and had done "a good deal of fowling". In his oral statement he told Timoney his gun had been confiscated by the Black-and-Tans, a common occurrence then. The interval between the two shots "was just while you would be moving your finger from one trigger to the other and taking quick aim again...".

Explaining that he knew the locality well, Moloney said the shots came from the direction of Caesar's house. "There was a slight breeze blowing from that direction...This was about 9.25 a.m." The bell for morning Mass was ringing when he heard the two shots. (This was shortly before Gleeson found the body of the murdered woman). Pat Coman told him he also heard the two shots. Moloney first heard of Moll Carthy's death around midday that day, but did not know she had been shot until he attended the inquest the next day. When he heard her clothes were dry after Wednesday night's rain, he concluded that the two shots he heard were the ones that killed her. Some days later he told his story to Fr. O'Malley, who told him to tell the Guards: "I told him I would not". In January, after Gleeson was returned for trial, Moloney again spoke to Fr. O'Malley about the shots. The latter now told him "not to bother about it, as it was of no importance, and it was on the Wednesday she was killed". A shorter statement which Timoney obtained from Fr. O'Malley confirmed Moloney's story. The latter came to him one night soon after the murder and told him of having heard two shots as the bell for Mass was ringing around 9.25 a.m. on Thursday. He told Moloney to tell the Guards. "He told me he would not...and warned me not to tell anyone what he had told me". The priest also recalled a conversation he had with Moloney at the church gate in January 1941 about the trial, but could not now remember the exact conversation. He regarded Moloney as truthful. Timoney read this statement to Fr. O'Malley in his home on 25 March. The priest agreed it was correct, but refused to sign it.

Patrick Coman said he too was a farmer in Lough Kent, 66 years old, and had lived there all his life. Around 9.30 a.m. on the Thursday, while standing in the paddock behind his house, he heard two shots in quick succession from the Marlhill direction. The following evening Moloney told him he heard them too. While searching for John Fitzgerald Timoney met Michael Long, who said he was employed by Fitzgerald. Timoney asked him about the shots fired at a cat, and Long remembered that on the evening of Wednesday 20 November Fitzgerald fired one shot at a cat in a tree. It fell off and was killed with a stick by Edmond Barrett, another employee. Fitzgerald, according to Long, took in the gun soon after the single shot because it got too dark for shooting. However, when Timoney first met Long he said two shots had been fired. Barrett told Timoney the same story, but also altered it when asked to make a signed statement. Both were employees of Fitzgerald, who then introduced himself to Timoney as a 70-year-old farmer. At about 5.45 p.m. on Wednesday 20 November he fired at a cat in a tree. "I did not fire a second shot at the cat, or at all that evening".

Harry Gleeson's appeal took four days in the Court of Criminal Appeal – from 31 March to 3 April 1941. This court consists of one Supreme Court and two High Court judges. In Gleeson's case its members were Chief Justice Timothy Sullivan; the president of the High Court, Mr. Justice Conor Maguire (not related to Mr. Justice Martin Maguire); and Mr. Justice Henry Hanna. An appeal to this court is based on the official transcript of the trial and on any new evidence allowed by the court. Only one judgement, that of the majority, is given. No official record is kept of arguments made in the appeal court. All that has survived are the copy of the judgement and some private notes of judges and (among the MacBride papers) of the defence barristers. The only substantial press report of the Gleeson appeal appeared in the *Tipperary Star*.

From MacBride's papers one can get some idea of the cases made by both sides. They show extensive research done by the defence team in the four weeks between trial and appeal. A list of 25 cases is headed "Misdirection Cases". A page from a Law Library notebook headed "Judge is bound to put defence to jury" contains eleven English cases dating from 1909 to 1931. There are also summaries of decisions in 22 more cases, among them the famous Malahide murder case of 1926. From other notes it is clear what were some of the points MacBride or Nolan-Whelan intended to make at the hearing. "Judge should not put question to witness suggesting that he [judge] is satisfied with the defendant's guilt"; "nondirection as to parts of defence may amount to misdirection"; "judge must not put himself in the position of the jury on questions of fact".

Nolan-Whelan took two days to put Gleeson's case. On the third day MacBride concentrated on the new evidence. Whelan's main argument was that Maguire's presentation of the defence was inadequate; he gave examples from the transcript. MacBride explained the substance and effect of the new evidence which Gleeson's solicitor had acquired since the trial. Joseph A. McCarthy SC suggested that the dead woman's clothes could have dried out by the time of Dr. O'Connor's examination near midday, or that the body might have been covered all night. Neither possibility had been raised at the trial. Murnaghan suggested that a sheet placed over the body for a couple of hours might account for the dry state of the clothes. He also argued that if a judge felt there was no reality in a defence he was not bound to put it to a jury. He claimed that there was no evidence to support the theory of a Thursday morning killing; this, he argued, was based on speculation.

When McCarthy argued that Gleeson was the father of the last Carthy child it seems from MacBride's notes that he ran into trouble with the bench. "Jos. A. stopped short then" is MacBride's wry comment. The Chief Justice queried McCarthy on what seemed to him to be defects in the State's ballistics evidence; he suggested that the jury should not have convicted Gleeson unless the two cartridges had been produced that had been used to kill Moll Carthy. Mr. Justice Hanna, the leading criminal lawyer on the court, intervened several times during Nolan-Whelan's presentation on the first day. His comments tended to defend the trial judge's charge about the State's failure to call the Caesars as witnesses, since it was open to the defence to call them. Regarding the quarrel between the two boys and Gleeson in the yard, Hanna said he found it difficult to understand Gleeson's poor memory of the event. He pointed out that when the two boys were in the box they were not asked about

68

this quarrel by defence lawyers, who could also have asked for their recall after Supt. Mahony's evidence.

For technical legal reasons, Gleeson's hope of winning the appeal were slim, and the admittedly skimpy account of the hearing suggests that his lawyers did not get a sympathetic hearing. It can hardly have been a surprise to them when on 8 April the court announced its decision and dismissed Gleeson's appeal. What might have surprised them was the brevity of the judgement. It contains only 2,500 words, and cannot have taken the Chief Justice more than ten minutes to deliver. The court found that none of the three main grounds of appeal – the trial judge's charge, his admission of Supt. Mahony's evidence of the scene in McCarthy's yard and the availability of new evidence – had been established. That afternoon, a mile away in Mountjoy jail, Harry Gleeson was playing cards with two warders when a third entered his cell. "Harry, I'm afraid I have bad news for you". "Just as I expected", commented Gleeson as the cards were collected and put away.

The first two pages of the judgement, which in total runs to little over seven typed foolscap pages, summarise the facts and the arguments. It then concludes that the omission from the charge of any reference to the dry state of the dead woman's clothes was not "of such a grave nature as would justify the Court in quashing the conviction". As to the objections to Supt. Mahony's evidence, the court, while admitting "that it would have been more...proper to have examined the McCarthys as to the conversation", held that this defect did not make the evidence inadmissible. Reviewing the third ground of appeal (the new evidence), the Chief Justice summarised in one sentence the fresh testimony and then referred with equal brevity to a 1937 decision, that the court could decide whether or not to admit new evidence either after having heard a summary of it, or after hearing the evidence of the proposed witnesses. It ruled that in Gleeson's case the new evidence was inconsistent with that already given, and found this view confirmed by both Gleeson and Reid, who said they heard no shots on the Thursday morning. In these circumstances, Chief Justice Sullivan concluded, "this Court is of opinion that no reasonable jury should be influenced by the evidence of Moloney and Coman "in arriving at a conclusion as to the time at which Mary McCarthy was murdered". The date of Gleeson's execution was re-fixed at 23 April, less than three weeks away. A striking omission from the judgement is any reference to the ballistics evidence, on which so much of the State's case depended. About two of the ten days were occupied by this evidence, much of it given by police experts, one of them cross-examined at great length. Yet not a single word appears in the appeal court's judgement about this vital testimony. Could it be that none of the three judges understood its vital importance, as one suspects the jury didn't either?

His appeal now lost, Harry Gleeson still had two more chances to escape the hangman's noose. He could either appeal to the Supreme Court or ask the Government for a reprieve. To appeal to the Supreme Court, his lawyers had to get a certificate from the Attorney General that the appeal court decision involved one or more "points of law of exceptional interest", and that an appeal was "desirable in the public interest". On 15 April, eight days before he was due to hang, Gleeson's solicitor applied for this certificate. Timoney included a sixteen-page memorandum drafted by the barristers, listing 25 matters on which it was claimed that Maguire's charge was defective. Within twenty-four hours the Attorney General, Kevin Haugh SC (later a High and Supreme Court judge) refused the certificate to Gleeson. His solicitor at once began a reprieve campaign by ordering several thousand copies of a petition from the *Tipperary Star* newspaper in Thurles.

Using a network of friends of the Gleeson family, this campaign was organised on a parish and town basis in County Tipperary. Soon 4,000 signatures had been collected and sent to the Minister for Justice. A later parish priest of New Inn, Fr. Timothy Murnane, estimated that the eventual total was over 7,000. As recently as the Summer of 1992 I met a friend of Gleeson who claimed that from a remote Tipperary village he had personally collected over 2,000 signatures. From Timoney's file it is clear that Sean MacBride used political associates to promote the reprieve campaign. From letters and lists that have survived it is also clear that support for Gleeson crossed political boundaries. Among those who signed the petition were Col. Jerry Ryan (Fine Gael), a prominent figure of the 1918-1923 period, Padraig O Glasain, the chairman of Thurles Urban Council, two leading Tipperary solicitors, Robin Frewen and James Darcy, and the Abbot of Roscrea Abbey, Fr. Ailbe O. Cist.

The Taoiseach, Eamonn de Valera, agreed (under pressure from an old friend, the rugby international Mike Ryan of Cashel), to receive a deputation to discuss a reprieve for Gleeson. In his office in Government Buildings in Dublin de Valera, accompanied by Chief Superintendent Sheridan and Superintendent Mahony, received the group from Tipperary. He explained to them that he had asked the Chief Supt. to examine the entire file of the case and to give him a solemn assurance that Gleeson had been correctly convicted, if that were the case. "I have received that assurance, gentlemen", he told Ryan; "what more can I do?" So confident were those appointed to meet de Valera that he would find in Gleeson's favour that several of them did not even bother to travel to Dublin. On 15 April Gleeson's solicitor sent the Minister for Justice a 25-page memorandum in support of the petition. Using a minimum of legal jargon, he dealt with the case from the layman's angle, trying to win the Minister's sympathy by showing the unsatisfactory nature of the trial.

PETITION FOR REPRIEVE OF HENRY GLEESON

WE, the undersigned, hereby humbly request the Government, pursuant to the provisions of the Constitution of Ireland, to advise the President to commute the sentence of death passed upon Henry Gleeson in the Central Criminal Court on the 27th day of March, 1941.

NAME	ADDRESS

NOTE—The execution has been fixed for the 23rd April, 1941, and, accordingly, it is essential that all Reprieve Forms should reach Henry Gleeson's Solicitor, Mr. JOHN J. TIMONEY, LL.B., St. Michael's Street, Tipperary, as soon as possible.

Original copy of Petition for Reprieve of Henry Gleeson.

New evidence that had been uncovered since the appeal is mentioned for the first time in this memorandum. Contact had been resumed between the two younger Carthy children and Miss Cooney. She was told by Michael and Mary that, when on the Wednesday night Patrick (the older boy) had gone out searching for his mother, he had brought a lantern with him, and was satisfied that her body (or her dog) was not in the spot where it was found by Gleeson the next morning. Patrick had not given this evidence to either court. Finally, on Good Friday 19 April MacBride sent a personal handwritten letter to the Minister for Justice, Mr. Gerry Boland, whom he had known in the 1918-1924 period, enclosing copies of the fresh evidence. "Gleeson's solicitor believed he had not been told the whole truth about the shots fired at the cat", wrote MacBride, who explained that "Fitzgerald's yard, where these shots had been fired, was much nearer to the place where Hennessy [the only known person who heard the two Wednesday evening shots] was when he said he heard them".

In a single-sentence letter dated 19 April – before Boland could have opened MacBride's letter – a junior official of the Dept. of Justice, Peter Berry, later to achieve fame as the Secretary of the Dept. during the 1970 arms trial, informed Timoney that "it has been decided that a reprieve cannot be granted, and that accordingly the law must take its course" in four days time. Harry Gleeson was hanged on 23 April 1941.

As the Spring of 1941 gave way to early Summer, the people of New Inn began to return to normality after five months of suppressed tension. But the murder and its awful consequences could not easily be forgotten. As well as Moll, another man who for twenty years had lived among them – working, hurling, playing his fiddle and breeding greyhounds – was gone from them. In the case of The People versus Henry Gleeson the law had taken its course. For some people in New Inn, however, especially those who had been closest to him, it proved difficult to accept that Harry Gleeson had been the killer of Moll Carthy. For the Caesar household, life was changed for ever. Although his brother Pat soon took Harry's place, the two elderly Caesars understandably found it hard to come to terms with what had happened. Deeply religious though both were, they could not forgive some of their neighbours who had, as the Caesars saw it, by giving evidence against Harry helped to send him to his death. Some others, it is true, convinced of his innocence, rallied round; but the only result of their loyalty was to divide the local people on the murder.

Around the farm at Marlhill plenty of evidence still remained of the Caesar's dead nephew – his greyhounds and his beloved fiddle, for example. One day Mrs Caesar, determined that nobody else would ever play Harry's instrument, brought it out to a remote spot on the farm and buried it under a tree. Some time later she had an unexpected visitor, when a police car drew up in the yard. Supt. Mahony had been given the delicate task of returning Harry's clothes, sent back from Mountjoy jail. An angry confrontation followed at the front door, with the police officer having to leave hastily as the old woman showered imprecations on him. The Supt. could at least retreat to the comparative security of Cahir station. For Sergt. Daly there was no choice but to stick it out in New Inn, with nearly another seven years to go before retirement. Rumours and counter-rumours about him began to circulate as thickly as the rain clouds over the Galtee Mountains. As the local officer in charge of the case, his role continued to come under almost daily scrutiny, with his armchair critics divided into two camps. Some assumed he had been duped by the real killer or killers; others suspected he had actually been privy to their plans.

The sergeant's position did not improve when it became apparent that an official enquiry into the case had begun. Plain-clothes Guards from Dublin came and went, and it was observed that most of those interviewed were friends of Daly. In one case the sergeant got in first, pleading with a man for whom he had done some minor illicit favours to stand by him if asked for a character reference. There was also a curious visit to Caesar's land by Sergt. Reynolds and Guard Scully (but not by Daly) with Patrick McCarthy as late as Easter Sunday, only ten days before Gleeson was due to die, and after he had lost his appeal. According to Patrick, he once again pointed out the spot he reached on his midnight search for his mother. Why at that late stage, people asked? As rumours persisted that somehow Sergt. Daly had had some involvement in the plan to rid New Inn of Moll Carthy, the parish priest, a friend of Daly, intervened. From the pulpit he warned parishioners about mischievous speculation and rejected allegations against Daly. However, just as his own predecessor's sermon years earlier had little effect on Moll herself, Fr. O'Malley's warning won Daly little respite from the gossip.

Fr. O'Malley's public intervention switched discussion round to his own low-key role in the Gleeson affair. Advocates of the Thursday morning theory doubtless prised out of the retired tailor Joseph Moloney the fact that the parish priest, when twice confided in about the morning shots, had discouraged further inquiry into what both Joseph Moloney and Patrick Coman insisted they had heard. Reid's story, that Fr. O'Malley had urged him not to pursue his complaint against the Guards until the murder case was over, was also probably recalled. This advice, Reid told his solicitor, he took to mean he would be wasting his time ever going to law against the Guards. How, some people wondered, could Fr. O'Malley be so sure of this? Even more serious for the Guards was the story that now began to spread, about Patrick McCarthy having brought a lamp with him on his late-night search of the fields for his missing mother and of finding neither mother nor dog where Gleeson found them both next morning.

Moll was known to snare rabbits in large quantities. After dark was the normal time for checking snares, and this could not normally be done without a lamp. All this, some locals realised with apprehension, lent still more support to the Thursday morning theory.

The importance of this new information cannot be exaggerated. If it were true and had been available at the trial, it would probably have demolished the prosecution case for a Wednesday night killing. Alternatively, if it were proved untrue, it would have cast doubt on the whole of Patrick's evidence; how could a jury be sure anything else he said was true? And if he were an unreliable witness, what about his much younger brother Michael? One may be sure that, on hearing this startling story, Miss Cooney passed it on to Fr. O'Malley. If he in turn told the Guards, this would explain Patrick's trip on Easter morning out to Caesar's farm with the two Guards – perhaps without the knowledge of Sergt. Daly? Naturally Gleeson's solicitor also heard all about this. During the Summer and Autumn of 1941 he tried without success to meet Patrick McCarthy. When he eventually caught up with him, nearly a year after the murder, the boy denied the whole story, and when challenged by the solicitor to record his denial in a sworn statement, he did so. However, this cut no ice with Miss Cooney, nor with some of the local people, who insist to this day that a household like the Carthys engaged in nocturnal rabbit-snaring could not have been able to manage without a lamp. Could Patrick's denial have been an attempt by the Guards to dissuade Timoney from continuing to probe the whole affair?

As for the younger McCarthy children, with their home now broken up, District Justice Troy at a court sitting on 9 May 1941 directed their committal to State care. With Patrick living and working away from home, the Carthy cottage began to fall into disrepair. Today nothing is left but parts of two walls. The law also moved against old John Caesar with what seems like unusual haste. In June 1941 Supt. Mahony formally revoked his firearms licence. When asked for the reason by Caesar's solicitor, the Supt. simply quoted the Firearms Act of 1925, and said that in his view Caesar was "a person who cannot be permitted to have a firearm in his possession without danger to public safety and the peace". Caesar was then in his seventies and never used the gun except to kill vermin on his own land. Under pressure from the solicitor, Mahony changed his mind about confiscating the weapon and allowed Caesar to sell it privately.

Tommy Reid, who had lived with the Caesars since he was seventeen, also left New Inn, apparently because of the effect the whole affair had on him. After the jury's verdict he took ill, apparently a nervous reaction, and had to spend some time resting with an aunt in Dublin. He was to spend much of his later life in Dublin. Then ten years after Gleeson's hanging Caesar himself died in his 84th year, followed some years later by his wife.

74

The farm continued to be worked by Harry's brother Pat, until his death a bachelor in the 1970s. A new owner then moved in and the house and outbuildings were demolished. Ironically, with all the fences now levelled and the hedges removed too, the only sign today of the Caesar farm is one of the two pumps Moll used to draw water from.

K/OD   Tipperary. Thursday, May, 1st. 1941.

John Ceasar, Esq.,
Marlhill,
New Inn,
Cahir,
Co. Tipperary.

Dear Mr. Ceasar,

I asked Thomas Reid when he called here to-day if you had got my letter to you of April, 24th. 1941. He told me you had got it but he had no knowledge of your having got the copy of Mr. MacBride's letter to me of April, 23rd., 1941, which was enclosed with my letter of April, 14th. I am to-day sending you a copy of Mr. MacBride's letter and also a copy of my letter to you of the 24th. ultimo.

In view of the contents of Mr. MacBride's letter I felt that Thomas Reid would have known of it if it had reached you. That is the reason I am sending to you this second copy.

I think you need have no doubt but that some day Harry's name will be cleared and his innocence established and you already have my assurance and Mr. MacBride's assurance that we will leave nothing in our power undone to achieve this as we both believe fully in Harry's innocence.

Yours sincerely,
John J. Timoney.

Copy of letter from John Timoney to John Caesar.

Chapter 7

A fair trial?

Whether he was innocent or guilty of the murder of Moll Carthy, Harry Gleeson was entitled to a fair trial. In this chapter, using only the official record of the trial, it will be shown that he did not get a fair trial, and that from start to finish the conduct of his trial was biased. Important portions of the evidence given against Gleeson were presented in an unfair, deceptive or dishonest way. Vital evidence was deliberately concealed, withheld or suppressed by the prosecution. Most serious of all, by his handling of the trial, the trial judge, mainly (but by no means exclusively) through his address to the jury after the evidence had concluded, behaved so partially that he effectively denied Gleeson a fair trial.

On 30 November 1940 Harry Gleeson was charged with the murder on 20 November of Mary McCarthy. When his trial opened almost two months later the prosecution was permitted by the judge to alter the charge to "on or about the 20th or 21st day of November". After initial opposition Gleeson's lawyer consented to the change. As a result of the alteration to the charge, Gleeson's lawyers were suddenly faced with what, strictly speaking, was a different charge from the one they had been prepared for, and employed by Gleeson to defend. Nolan-Whelan's consent to the change of date may have been a public relations gesture to the jury, faced with a judge whom he correctly surmised would grant the request for the change anyway. In hindsight, however, it was a tactical error by the defence and should have been raised at the appeal, where it was overlooked. The reason for the change of date was obvious. For a considerable time after the discovery of the murdered woman's body the Guards were unable to decide whether Moll Carthy had been killed on the Wednesday evening or on the Thursday morning. It was because of this uncertainty that they spent over twelve hours on 25 November questioning Gleeson's fellow-employee Reid. They tried to persuade him to agree that Gleeson had been up and out early on Thursday and was returning to bed, instead of, as Reid had insisted, merely coming upstairs to wake him after having lit the fire and prepared breakfast.

Particularly in a capital case, a long-standing rule of law requires all relevant evidence in the prosecution's possession to be disclosed to the defence before the trial. One of the most serious breaches of this rule in Gleeson's case concerned twelve-year-old Michael McCarthy. His evidence contained inconsistencies and differed from that of his sister Mary. Yet, despite repeated requests by Gleeson's solicitor, the Chief State Solicitor refused to supply a copy of any statement made by the boy to the Guards. Other important information, relating to the vital question of when the fatal shots were fired, was also withheld from the defence, and only came to its knowledge after the trial was over. When Gleeson's solicitor investigated Joseph Moloney's story of the Thursday morning shots, it transpired that John Fitzgerald (the man who shot the cat the previous evening) had reported this shooting to Sergt. Daly as early as 21 November, the day the body was found. This means that long before the case got to court Daly knew about the possibility that it was the Thursday morning shots, rather than those Thomas Hennessy said he heard the previous evening, that had killed Moll Carthy. Assuming Daly passed on Fitzgerald's story to his superiors, someone in authority neglected to offer this evidence to the defence. If on the other hand Daly kept this information to himself (by, for example, not making a record of it) the result was the same – to lessen Gleeson's chance of getting a fair trial.

Probably the most serious example of undisclosed evidence related to the purchase of ammunition by John Caesar. A vital link in the State's chain of evidence was proof that Moll Carthy died from injuries caused by cartridges fired from Caesar's gun, the only such weapon available to Gleeson and one he and his uncle used to control vermin on the farm. In such circumstances the law requires the best available evidence, in Gleeson's case simply the production in court of the firearms register required to be kept by the local firearms dealer. At the trial an employee of Feehan's hardware store in Cashel said that on 10 October 1940 John Caesar had bought a box of 25 cartridges. He also said he had not brought the firearms register with him; instead he produced a receipt for the sale. Although Mr Justice Maguire directed the register to be produced the next day, it was never produced. As a result, the mass of ballistics evidence later given by the Guards proceeded without anybody ever being told what type or size of cartridge had killed Moll Carthy. Yet the obvious person who could have supplied this information, John Caesar himself, sat in court for the entire 10 days but was never called as a witness. Just what Feehan's register shows (and does not show) has already been told in Chapter 4. Moreover, when Gleeson's solicitor visited Feehan to see the register he met with a blunt refusal from Feehan, who told him that although his employee Leamy had been summoned as a witness, he had not been directed by the Guards to bring the register to Dublin.

By far the worst offender in denying Gleeson a fair trial was the judge himself. In other words, the person charged by law with ensuring an impartial hearing played a major part in sending Gleeson to the gallows. Moreover, Maguire's partiality was not confined to his address to the jury. Almost from the opening of the trial he showed an apparent bias against the accused man, his lawyers and his witnesses. Criticism of the defence case came intermittently from the bench; in contrast, prosecution witnesses were praised and even at times defended from criticism by Nolan-Whelan or MacBride. Maguire's attitudes to the two principal medical witnesses reveal a striking difference. Dr. McGrath for the State was listened to with respect. To Dr. Flood for the defence he put questions that tended to challenge the correctness of his opinions. They also tended to lessen any impact Flood might make on the jury, and gave the impression that, where there was any difference between McGrath and Flood, Maguire preferred the former, with the implication that the jury should do likewise.

In his relations with the opposing pairs of barristers Maguire also showed apparent signs of partiality. Nowhere in the whole of the transcript is there even one minor brush with Murnaghan, the junior State counsel. MacBride on the other hand was constantly subjected to interruptions, at times implying that his questions were unnecessary, improper or even wrongly phrased, and other times challenging his interpretations of earlier evidence and frequently breaking the flow of his cross-examination. Maguire's brusqueness was probably never more apparent than during the evidence of the first police witness, Guard Quinlan the mapper. Using maps which the defence's own expert (the architect Munden) had prepared, MacBride cross-examined Quinlan in great detail. He found himself constantly interrupted and harassed from the bench. Nevertheless he succeeded in showing up a major error in Quinlan's measurements; he had actually placed the body on the wrong side of a fence. This concession led the judge to tell the jury that he had often heard Quinlan give evidence, and he was always a trustworthy witness for the State. Several days later Maguire returned to this point, and in sarcastic language repeated his faith in Quinlan at a time when MacBride could not reply. When Munden gave evidence for the defence Maguire also repeated his praise of Quinlan.

During the vital evidence of Michael McCarthy, the dead woman's young son and possibly the State's most important witness, Maguire also displayed apparent bias. Doubtless the strain of a court appearance, the recall of the last day he saw his mother alive and the confrontation in court with Gleeson meant that Michael McCarthy was a hesitant, nervous witness from the start. Although gentle handling of the boy was required to elicit important facts from him, Maguire's treatment of him went close to actually helping him to tell his story. Yet to no less than 34 questions Michael gave no reply at all, and to a further thirteen a brief "I don't know". On 67 occasions during Michael's evidence the judge made some kind of intervention, either to the witness or to counsel. Whether intentionally or not, most of these breaks tended to help the boy. The judge's treatment of Michael McCarthy contrasts starkly with his interventions six days later when the accused man got into the box. Admittedly on Day 7 there were only four interventions from the bench. On Day 8, however, when Gleeson spent most of the day giving evidence, Maguire broke in on twenty-one separate occasions, all but one of them during McCarthy's cross-examination, when none (save perhaps of a minor nature) should have been called for. It is true that three of his interventions that day were critical of Joseph A. McCarthy SC, but unlike Maguire's questions to Michael McCarthy none of those put to Gleeson remotely helped his case and many were distinctly critical, some even hostile.

Several times during the evidence the judge even injected a note of sarcasm or flippancy into the proceedings, so much so that reading the transcript one has to remind oneself that a man's life was at stake. The farm labourer Michael Gayson was suddenly asked which of the Caesar household was the best shot. When Dr. Flood was explaining why he felt a proposition put by Dr. McGrath was invalid, Maguire broke in to ask Flood if he meant that the only way to test McGrath's theory would be to take a woman down to Tipperary, first shoot her and then blow her face away. On another occasion, when McCarthy was asking about the dead woman's life-style, Maguire asked: "Are you saying that this woman kept open house?" McCarthy's "Yes" only helped to build up for the jury a picture of an immoral woman, which, of course, tended to implicate Gleeson.

Despite Mr. Justice Maguire's many interventions during the presentation of evidence, it on his charge to the jury after the evidence concluded that proof of the allegation of an unfair trial largely rests. Much of his address read, and must have sounded, like one long selective attack on Gleeson. By the time it was over, the jury's verdict was predictable. What was surprising was its recommendation that Harry Gleeson should not hang. To help to put the charge into perspective, it took a day-and-a-half to deliver – about two hours on Day 9 and at least four more on Day 10. This does not include the short additional charge necessitated by Nolan-Whelan's objections. Maguire's address was based entirely on his own notes of the evidence. Obviously the quality of these depended on such factors as the speed of his handwriting, their subsequent legibility and, of course, the frequency of his own interruptions, during which he could hardly take notes. Comparison between the transcript and Maguire's charge reveals some significant differences.

Probably the part of the charge to which least objection could be taken was the opening thirty minutes or so. As might be expected from an experienced criminal lawyer, he gave a lucid explanation of the distinction between law and fact, the latter being for the jury to decide. Reminding them that the prosecution case depended entirely on circumstantial evidence, he emphasised that in its cumulative effect this was just as good as direct evidence; murder by its nature was "necessarily secretive". However, permeating the whole of the speech after the first half-hour is an implicit belief in Gleeson's guilt. In the case of many witnesses whose evidence he gave in summary, little or no information that came out in cross-examination was imparted. As a rough guide to the apparent priority in Maguire's mind to the defence case, it was not until page 89 of his 112-page address that he gave a summary of the case made for Gleeson – in a form similar to that which he had used to summarise the State case back on page 11. As Nolan-Whelan pointed out when the jury retired, this meant that the defence case was wholly inadequately put to the jury.

The defence theory that Moll Carthy was shot elsewhere and not near the Dug-Out Maguire described as "far-fetched" and "fantastic". As early as the first fifteen minutes of his speech he showed a complete disregard for the defence case that she was not killed where she was found.

"Someone must have gone to meet that woman somewhere in the neighbourhood of the Dug-Out: must have gone there with a gun: must have loaded it, must have waited for the victim, if the victim was not already there: must have fired and must have fired again, and these shots must have caught this unfortunate woman and caused her death".

Of the six (or seven?) assumptions in that sentence, at least three had been challenged either by the defence witnesses (including Gleeson himself) or by the defence's cross-examination of major State witnesses. There is no reference anywhere in the charge to the vital question as to when Moll Carthy was killed; Maguire appears to have regarded any time of death other than the Wednesday evening as out of the question. Neither Dr. O'Connor's evidence about the warmth of the body nor Dr. McGrath's surprise at Dr. O'Connor's finding was mentioned. Both would, of course, tend to support the Thursday morning theory. Early in his charge the judge told the jury to put the question of immorality out of their minds. They should not regard Moll as a person who hired herself out for immoral purposes, any more than they should conclude that she stole potatoes from her neighbours. All this was above criticism; had the rest of his speech been so balanced, there would have been much less ground for an appeal. However, he repeatedly failed to abide by his own rules.

In the course of his two-day speech every one of the forty-eight State witnesses got at least a brief mention by Maguire – even all the minor witnesses. From the first thirty or forty minutes onwards the charge amounted to almost a complete re-run of the previous seven days' evidence, but with a noticeable anti-defence bias. His treatment of Michael McCarthy's evidence is typical of Maguire's approach throughout. Because of its selectiveness it is distinctly sympathetic to the boy. It tended to over-emphasise his evidence about meetings between his mother and Gleeson. Also, by reminding the jury of the boy's account of visitors to his home in the evenings, it under-scored the prosecution's allegations of immorality. It is remarkable too for what it omitted. There was no mention at all of Michael's unanswered or inadequately answered questions. It stated that he could count to ten, but not that at twelve years he could not go any further than ten. It mentioned that the Carthys had a clock, but not that Michael could not read it. It reminded the jury that he had said that Sergt. Daly's visit was on Tuesday, but not that everyone else (including Daly) said it was on Wednesday. It recalled Michael saying he had got a sack from Halpin, but not that Halpin had denied it.

There were even some inaccuracies in Maguire's account of Michael's evidence. Twice he called James Condon "Tom". He used Munden's maps to explain to the jury what view Michael would have of certain fields, but neglected to point out that Munden said Michael would have had no such view. He claimed that Michael was afraid of Gleeson, although nobody had given evidence to this effect. Twice later he tried to justify or explain this remark, once suggesting that it was, perhaps, because of the confrontation in the yard that Michael had run back home when he saw Gleeson near the Dug-Out on Thursday morning. A more serious error came when Maguire near the end of his speech said there were no potatoes in McCarthys the day Moll went missing, and that her son Michael had sworn to this. In fact, although Michael had said this in the District Court, he did not repeat it at the trial.

A major omission from the judge's treatment of Michael McCarthy's evidence was his failure to mention that the State had not extracted from either boy his account of the confrontation in the yard witnessed by Supt. Mahony. Maguire's treatment of Patrick McCarthy was nearly as unsatisfactory as his account of Michael's testimony. He made no comment on the boy's midnight search for his missing mother, confining himself to a bland telescoped account of this event: it was clearly based on inadequate or illegible notes. When summarising Mary McCarthy's evidence, he repeated her story of Michael returning from school on Wednesday, but did not remind the jury that Michael had said he was not at school that day. It was at this stage in his speech that Mrs. Caesar made her protest from the gallery. The State's failure to call either her or her husband was a breach of its duty to put all the facts before the jury, something Maguire did not point out in his charge. It also constituted a tactical "stroke" by the State lawyers, because it forced Gleeson's counsel to make an agonising decision. Clearly, whatever weight the Caesars might carry with the jury had they been called by the State, as Gleeson's uncle and aunt they would have carried far less had they been called by the defence.

Once again there was a striking contrast between Maguire's account of Michael McCarthy's evidence and his treatment of Thomas Reid. In a manner that completely deprived his summary of objectivity, he began with some remarks that showed the jury what his opinion of Reid was. "He appeared...to give his evidence with some reluctance...due to slowness of speech and thought that you find...often in people associated with humble working positions on the land". Then, after he had gone through Reid's testimony and managed to convey his own disbelief in the allegations of police brutality, Maguire gave a short lecture to the jury on the right of the Guards to question people in the vicinity of a crime – and to get answers from them. Finally, as if stung by Reid's story of the assault on him in the police station, Maguire gave it as his firm conviction that every Guard who gave evidence in the case had "conducted the investigation with perfect fairness and propriety", ending with a verbal onslaught on lawyers who took "unbridled licence" to attack policemen doing their duties. Sergt. Daly's unexplained visit to the Carthy cottage, originally queried by the judge himself, was barely mentioned, and then in inaccurate terms: "I had seen her five or six times on the 20th November about 3.30 p.m.", something the transcript shows Daly never said. The State's failure to produce the firearms register, also first queried by Maguire himself, was dismissed in a single sentence.

The 112-page charge is spattered with minor factual errors, which cumulatively may have affected the jury, accustomed to taking a judge's accuracy for granted. Maguire told the jury that the journey from Carthy's to their neighbour Condon (a mere half-mile, as the map shows), took Michael thirty minutes by bicycle. Reading from his notes of Supt. Mahony's evidence, he said that when Caesar handed over his gun, "He got it in the kitchen." The transcript for Day 6 shows that what Mahony said was: "Yes, he took it from his own bedroom." This error supported the State case that the gun was left lying round the kitchen, where Gleeson would have easy access to it. Towards the end of his six-hour address Maguire began to ignore his own earlier advice to disregard the moral aspects of the case. When discussing a possible motive for the murder, he painted a pathetic picture of Moll Carthy as a social outcast who could not mix freely locally. Then he speculated on the possible dilemma facing Gleeson, using as the basis of his speculation allegations that had all been denied by Gleeson, giving an example of judicial partiality at its worst:

"If he was associating with Mary McCarthy, he couldn't very well do it openly, and if he was the father of the child...he was not going to let the world know about it...if he was carrying on immorally with her, he was not going to post it on the highways and by-ways...They were thrown together...himself and this woman, and they had known each other for 15 or 16 years...You may think that he thought of being finished with Mary McCarthy...He was in a difficult position...living there with his uncle and aunt without any contract...any tenure."

As to why Mr. Justice Maguire was so biased in this case, several possible reasons can be suggested. The brutality of the murder, together with the sordid background to the case, may have repelled him from the start and distorted his sense of impartiality. He may have been impressed by the strength of the prosecution case simply because several of the more important witnesses, such as Dr. McGrath, Guard Quinlan and Supt. Reynolds, were already well known to him. He may even have taken an irrational dislike to one or both of the defending counsel – Nolan-Whelan with his plodding but meticulous style of advocacy, or MacBride because of his courage in standing up to Maguire. More likely as a possible explanation of his apparent unfairness is Maguire's own background at the Bar, where for years he had been a leading prosecutor. He was neither the first nor the last Irish judge to regard police evidence as above criticism, nor the first to assume that because the Chief State Solicitor employs leading barristers, the State case is watertight and no genuine defence to it exists.

Several other factors also affected Gleeson's chances of a fair trial, over which neither prosecution nor defence had any control, and for which the judge cannot be blamed. Foremost among these was probably the unrepresentative nature of the jury at that time, selected by a panel system then in operation. Eligibility for jury service then depended on a minimum property qualification and, as a result, Dublin jurors tended to come mainly from the middle-classes. Moreover, it was practically impossible for women to be selected for juries at that time. A jury like that in Gleeson's case would be predominantly urban-oriented in composition, background and outlook, as well as being mainly middle-aged and male. Among the twelve on the Gleeson jury I could not find, from their home or business addresses and their stated occupations, any likely to have had first-hand knowledge of Gleeson's life-style. It is easy to give examples of how a Dublin juror might have been (indeed, was) misled in the Gleeson trial. He would not have distinguished between using a gun and firing it, as

Maguire's charge shows he could not either. (To use a gun meant simply carrying it, but not firing it). As a result, such a juror would either disbelieve or not understand some of the evidence. He would not appreciate that shooting vermin on Caesar's land by his neighbours did not require Caesar's permission, and would therefore have drawn the wrong conclusions from Maguire's inaccurate remark in his charge, implying that only the Caesar household would shoot over the farm "because no one else had a right to."

The average Dublin juror fifty years ago would have had a middle-class outlook on life. Whatever about his standards of business practice, when it came to moral and social issues he tended to be conservative in the extreme. He would look with distaste on any suggestion of moral deviance. Harry Gleeson had, after all, to wait for eight days before he got a chance to deny on oath the accusations of immorality levelled against him in the first few minutes of his trial. Dublin jurors would have been very conscious of the significance of the vital economic commodity of land in rural Ireland. From various sources – history, press reports of law cases, even popular fiction – there would have been a perception of countrymen as land hungry. The threat of loss of his expected inheritance stressed by the judge but never proved, since the Caesars did not get into the box, might have been regarded by a jury of city residents as a sufficient motive for Gleeson to commit murder.

Another factor that must have had a big influence in the case is the weight the jury gave to the conflicting medical evidence. In this respect Dr. McGrath had a headstart on Dr. Flood, because of his official position and his wider experience of law cases. In any event Flood, who was something of a maverick in his profession, had a dogmatic manner in court that would have made him less convincing than Dr. McGrath. Nor can Gleeson's hearing defect, overlooked for most of the trial, be forgotten. What was disputed was not its existence but its seriousness. The prosecution from the start went on the offensive by challenging Gleeson's good faith on this score, and were supported by the judge. Yet a careful reading of the transcript shows several places where Gleeson did not grasp what was being said. His solicitor's file shows that Gleeson's hearing impairment was brought to Timoney's notice from the start by the Caesars. He wrote a series of letters and made several phone-calls, to try to track down what medication Gleeson took. Eventually an aunt of Gleeson living in Dublin supplied the answer. For years Harry had been using a prescription in her name, so that Gleeson's name was not on the books of any Tipperary chemist. Possibly his lawyers felt it might be difficult to convince the jury of the truth on this point.

A final factor, which indirectly affected Gleeson's chance of a fair trial, was of course, his legal representation – whether or not he got good legal advice and was competently defended. There can be no doubt about how well his solicitor did his work. Called in only after Gleeson had made his two statements to the Guards, John Timoney proved competent in every respect. Even a cursory examination of his file shows how tirelessly he worked to get Gleeson off. The amount of documentation he produced single-handedly for the two barristers, the many interviews he conducted of anyone remotely connected with the affair, the numerous train and taxi journeys he made, and the robust way he stood up to police harassment, all speak for themselves. Sean MacBride also gave of his best, although then a very junior member of the Bar. He attended the District Court without a Senior Counsel. At the trial he excelled in cross-examination of the ballistics expert and the pathologist, and stood up to constant interruptions from a judge who, he later insisted, was out for a guilty verdict from the first day. A criticism I have heard in the New Inn area is of Gleeson's lawyers' failure to employ a gun expert. However, Timoney's file clearly shows that both barristers urged this step, and the absence of such a witness for the defence can only be explained in one of two ways. Either the Caesars simply could not afford such an expert, who would probably have had to come from England anyway; or else none was available.

Of Nolan-Whelan one cannot be so sure as of his junior colleague. He had only become a senior counsel in 1937, and his other interests suggest that his career at the Bar may not have been his top priority. In a letter written in 1978 by MacBride, he stated that at the time of the trial Whelan was in poor health and "not up to the heavy task involved in a case of this nature." I have confirmed privately that Whelan was unwell around this time. At times he might have been more aggressive. But when it came to making instant objections to the charge, and to articulating without notice the grounds for an appeal, he served his client well.

Chapter 8

Conspiracy of silence

The most convenient starting-point in an attempt to prove that Harry Gleeson was innocent is a letter written in 1978 by Sean MacBride to a niece of Gleeson nearly forty years after the murder. She learned of the crime for the first time on going through the papers of her mother, a sister of Harry, who had recently died. After recovering from the discovery that her uncle had been hanged, she wrote to MacBride. Why, if Gleeson was innocent, as MacBride had said in an interview in 1974 (a press report of which was among her mother's papers), was he convicted? In his reply MacBride gave five reasons why he believed there had been a miscarriage of justice. Three of these were an unfairly conducted trial, a biased judge and Nolan-Whelan's ill-health, already mentioned. The other two were that "...the brutal nature of the crime...distorted the sense of objectivity...[of] those involved in the prosecution and trial..." and that because "most of the people in New Inn were in some way involved with Mary McCarthy, they entered into a conspiracy of silence." To understand what MacBride meant by a conspiracy of silence one needs to appreciate the impact Moll Carthy had made on the community of New Inn for twenty years. By her unorthodox life-style she not only flaunted convention; she also had a disruptive effect on many families in the area. She had successfully defeated several efforts, starting with the attempt in 1926 to burn her home, to move her from the district. Also, as MacBride pointed out, many local people had been associated in some way with Moll, or affected by her, starting with the fathers of her children, their families and two local police sergeants.

From the day her body was found the people of New Inn closed ranks so solidly that the efforts of the Guards to find the real culprits were hampered, even thwarted. It was as if, now that she was gone, the local people wanted to blot out all memories of her from their lives. A popular local photograph of a hurling team that included Gleeson was removed from many New Inn homes; in one house his head was neatly cut out. Because of the background of immorality in the dead woman's life-style, Gleeson's solicitor, his family and his close friends also found themselves unable to get information locally that would help to establish Harry's innocence. Rather than become involved in the case in any way because it involved a woman with Moll Carthy's reputation, people hung back and withheld information from the Caesars and their friends working to clear Harry, just as they did with the Guards. As a result, as has already been shown, a week after her body was found the Guards still could not decide whether she was shot on the Wednesday evening or on the Thursday morning, despite having drafted in a force of nearly forty men and obtained immediate technical help from police headquarters in Dublin. Long after Gleeson was hanged, Supt. Mahony admitted this privately to Harry's solicitor. Not only that, but it seems likely that the real killers (who, it will be argued, were local residents), in an effort to put the blame on Gleeson, spread rumours that he had been associating with Moll. "No smoke without fire" became the order of the day, and in rural Ireland of 1940 a suggestion of immorality, once made, was nearly impossible to disprove. In these circumstances, most people in New Inn, even those with no connection with the dead woman, found it prudent to deny co-operation both to the Guards and the Caesars. The fact that the latter were not from New Inn did not help them.

From evidence given at the trial or in statements obtained by Gleeson's solicitor, there is no difficulty finding examples of the conspiracy of silence. Living close to the Caesars and Moll Carthy was John (Seanie) Ryan, the local blacksmith, who like Moll daily snared rabbits. It was only on 12 February that Gleeson's solicitor John Timoney succeeded in meeting him. Ryan's forge was a clearing-house for local gossip. He was, consequently, a mine of information about New Inn. He admitted that he had been out setting snares on the Wednesday afternoon from about 4.00 p.m. to 6.00 p.m. and gave Timoney some information about the two Wednesday evening shots that will be revealed later in this Chapter. However, at the end of the interview, according to Timoney's notes, Ryan said: "I don't want to be mixed up in this case. I know nothing and I don't want to say anything...I have enough to do to mind my own business, and I'd sooner people weren't coming here asking me questions. I know you have to do your job, but I don't want to have anything to do between these people." Not surprisingly the Guards, who also interviewed Ryan, did not even serve a witness's summons on him; presumably they found him as unhelpful as did Timoney. One wonders how Ryan felt the day Gleeson was hanged, knowing (as I am convinced he did) that he had withheld vital information about the two shots Thomas Hennessy said he heard.

On Timoney's file too is a detailed statement taken on 25 March from the retired tailor Joseph Moloney, the man who said he heard the Thursday morning shots. Initially Moloney was reluctant to talk at all, until

Timoney persuaded him he might have information on which Gleeson's life might depend. Describing the circumstances in which he heard the morning shots, Moloney continued: "...I told him [Fr. O'Malley] I would not do so. I did not tell the Guards...because I did not want to become involved in the case in any way". Moloney's attitude reveals another aspect of the conspiracy of silence; it is likely that some local people were expecting neighbours to volunteer information first to the Guards or the Caesars, with the result that in the end none of them came forward. Miss Cooney, a person in whom people would confide, believed from her enquiries that a number of other people in the locality in addition to Moloney and Coman heard the Thursday morning shots.

Two more examples of the conspiracy of silence come from the evidence at the trial given by two New Inn men, friends of Gleeson and the Caesars summoned to give evidence for the State. The first, James Condon, was the man who brought his goat to Carthys on Wednesday afternoon and from whom Michael McCarthy later collected milk. When asked if he had gone to Moll's house, Condon said he hadn't; he had merely gone to her house with a goat, a subtle distinction that was probably lost on both the judge and jury. Asked by the judge if he had gone into Moll's house, Condon replied that he hadn't; he had passed by the door. Finally, when asked if he had paid Moll for her goat's services, he explained that payment was made by Mrs. Condon when the boy later came to them for the milk. The whole tenor of Condon's evidence showed anxiety to stress that it was his practice never to have any contact with the dead woman. Even more remarkable was testimony given the same day by John Halpin, the elderly farmer whose land adjoined both Caesar's and Moll's. Admitting he had known her all his life – he could have hardly sworn otherwise – he described the scene at Caesar's field pump where the young Carthys were lined up while Moll and Gleeson chatted, as seen from across the fence from Halpin's own land. Asked if he had joined in the conversation, Halpin said he hadn't: "I went on about my business." Under cross-examination he admitted that Moll had often got potatoes from his house, but they were given her by his wife – and he used to leave the house while Mrs. Halpin was doing so. In cross-examination Halpin agreed that his wife used also give potatoes to the Carthy children; this, he added, was done without his permission. When asked about the conversation with Gleeson the day Halpin advised him not to permit Moll to use the field pump, Halpin explained that his motive in urging Gleeson to get her to use the pump in the yard was for fear of the scandal that might arise "because of the previous pedigree of this woman." Yet, he admitted, he himself had offered her employment as a potato-picker in 1939.

In fairness to these local people, however, who withheld what some at least must have realised was important information about the murder, they only did what their spiritual leaders also did. Timoney met Fr. O'Malley at least three times about the Carthy affair. The purpose of his second meeting on 6 February, when Sean MacBride accompanied him, was to persuade the priest to give evidence about Gleeson's good character. In this he failed, as had Mrs. Caesar before him, despite her long friendship with Fr. O'Malley. The meeting, which lasted an hour, was, however, a friendly one. Despite his refusal to testify, the priest said he had a high opinion of Gleeson; so, he added, had Miss Cooney. He told Timoney about Reid's complaint to him about his beating by the Guards, and admitted that when Reid came to him a day after the event his left eye was still "bluish". Seven weeks later on 25 March, the day Timoney took the other statements about the Wednesday evening and Thursday morning shots, the solicitor was back in the parochial house, this time to ask Fr. O'Malley to confirm that Joseph Moloney had told him about the Thursday shots. The priest told Timoney he had urged Moloney to go to the Guards, but "he told me he would not...and warned me not to tell anyone what he had told me." The parish priest agreed he regarded Moloney as truthful. Timoney then read the statement over to him; Fr. O'Malley agreed it was correct, but refused to sign it. "He did not", according to Timoney's note of the interview, "wish to have anything to do with it." Timoney was then introduced to the curate, Fr. Denis Blackburn, who had visited the spot where the body lay the morning it was found. He told Timoney he knew neither Moll nor Gleeson, but also that he knew nothing against Harry morally. "I don't want to have anything to do with giving evidence in this case", he concluded, ending the meeting after ten minutes.

The conspiracy of silence even continued after Gleeson was hanged. During the summer of 1941, while preparing Reid's impending action for assault against two police officers (both named Reynolds), Timoney interviewed several local people who had seen the effects of the beating on Reid's face. Almost without exception, they either declined to give evidence or adopted an evasive attitude when asked if they would come to court. Yet all these people were lifelong friends of Reid; some had even encouraged him to go to law. One, Fr. O'Malley, had felt so strongly about what he had heard (from some of the others) that he had asked that Reid be sent up to him in his house. Fr. O'Malley was also involved in another episode which, in effect, deprived the defence of useful evidence, and which reveals a further aspect of the conspiracy of silence. Faced with conflicting stories in the District Court regarding Michael McCarthy's attendance or non-attendance at school on the Wednesday his mother went missing, Gleeson's solicitor (on advice from Nolan-Whelan) made two attempts to see the school roll. On his second visit on 6 February he met the principal, who refused to produce the roll-book without permission from her manager, the parish priest. She did, however, confirm Michael's attendance, as did her assistant, whom Timoney also met. Curiously, he appears not to have mentioned this topic to Fr. O'Malley, but his failure to serve witness-summonses on either teacher (as Nolan-Whelan also advised) suggests that he felt that without the roll-book neither teacher could help the defence. Presumably Fr. O'Malley simply did not want his school or its staff mixed up in the case.

One's first impression is that the only reason Gleeson was charged with the murder was because, as Moll Carthy's next-door neighbour, he was a more obvious suspect than most others in the locality. But, unless he had been having an immoral relationship with her, he had, after all, no motive for killing her. If, on the other hand, he had had such a relationship the Guards should have no difficulty in learning of it. Yet at the trial the only people to come forward and swear to an affair were the dead woman's three children. In the whole of New Inn nobody else could be found to support the children's allegation. However, to have an affair with Moll (or any other woman in New Inn) was simply not possible in the life led by Harry Gleeson. Not one of the fathers of Moll's six surviving children had been able to conceal his identity; if Gleeson had been having an affair with her, the whole of New Inn would have known. His every day was regulated as if by clockwork; ironically, it was this very routine that led to his discovery of the body – no accident, as will shortly be argued. So far from his early retirement to bed on the Wednesday night being exceptional, this was a common habit of Gleeson. His partner in the joint harvesting operation venture of 1940 (who is still alive) told Gleeson's solicitor that Harry often went to bed early, even when there were visitors in the house. So did a neighbour of Gleeson. The names of both are on Timoney's file, but neither was called as a witness, even though one sat through the trial.

As it was obvious locally that the day was approaching when Gleeson would take over the Caesar farm, it was easy to suggest the danger of loss of his inheritance as a motive. So far as the Guards were concerned, it seems that anything that might suggest that Gleeson was not the murderer was ignored. To give only two examples, it mattered little that he had never had a permanent relationship with a woman, nor that in the time available to him on the Wednesday evening he could not have got back home with hands, clothes, boots, and shotgun all covered with blood, washed it all off (and possibly even changed clothes), to sit down calmly to his evening meal, as Reid said he did. The fact that, like the Caesars and their neighbours, he had supplied the dead woman with potatoes, instead of suggesting charity or compassion, became in the eyes of the Guards part of a plot to meet her alone in his uncle's field. Near the village was a secluded spot near a quarry where, to this day, it is recalled that Moll used to meet men; why, if he was the killer, did Gleeson not pick this place rather than a spot close to home?

Nobody in New Inn was closer to Moll Carthy than Anna Cooney. Had Harry Gleeson been having an affair with Moll, or had he been the father of any of her children, Miss Cooney would have known. Yet she never suggested to anyone in New Inn that there was any association between the two; on the contrary, as Fr. O'Malley told Timoney and MacBride, she thought well of Harry. Nor is this all. In a letter (already mentioned) which she wrote to the Minister for Justice after Gleeson lost his appeal, Miss Cooney referred in some detail to the paternity of the Carthy children. Writing from the home in Rathgar, Dublin of her brother-in-law, District Justice John H. Rice, where she stayed while she attended every day of the ten-day trial, she implicitly exculpated Gleeson from responsibility for any of Moll's offspring; she "felt bound to communicate this information" to him, she told the Minister. She wrote: "...although Mary McCarthy told me who the fathers of her children were, she at no time mentioned Gleeson in this or any other connection. She did not tell me who the father of the last child was, and evaded my questions on the matter. Before this case I never heard Gleeson's name mentioned by anyone as being in any way connected with Mary McCarthy. I did hear the names of two other men mentioned as being likely fathers of the last child."

Miss Cooney's statement that Moll would not divulge the identity of her last child's father agrees with information the solicitor Timoney obtained from another source. When trying to arrange a meeting with the elusive John Ryan, the New Inn blacksmith, he interviewed Ryan's brother Patrick, also a blacksmith, who lived near Cashel. Patrick told the solicitor that he had heard that Moll had refused to tell anybody who was the father of the last child, and that she said his identity was a secret she would carry with her to the grave – as she apparently did. One of the two men mentioned by Miss Cooney as a likely father of the last child was questioned by the Guards at his home near Cashel, and was also interviewed by Timoney before the trial. He admitted he had been friendly with Moll, but denied any impropriety. He told Timoney that some years earlier, when he was evicted from his home, he and his wife had lodged with Moll for a couple of weeks. He continued: "I was blamed as the father of one of her children. I think it was _____'s [surname deleted] child. I didn't care what the people blamed me for, because I wasn't the father of any of her children. I was in her house many a time, and I never saw Gleeson there...I never heard of Gleeson having had anything to do with Moll..."

The surname deleted was the same as that of one of the two local men regarded by Miss Cooney as a likely father of Moll's last child. In Co. Tipperary, as in many parts of rural Ireland at the time, it was the custom for a priest to call on a parishioner known to have been the father of a recently-born child of an unmarried mother. No such visit was ever paid to the Caesar home, a fact Gleeson stressed in one of his conversations with Supt. Mahony – not recorded by Mahony, but noted down by Timoney as repeated to him by his client after the conversation. The significance of Miss Cooney's conviction that Harry was not the father of Moll's last child cannot be exaggerated, because if she was right Gleeson had no motive for killing Moll.

Harry Gleeson was framed by the real murderers simply because he was the ideal person for this purpose. A man of habit, he was known to walk his dogs early every morning by the same route. A body left on this route was bound to be found by him, and found by him at an hour in the winter when nobody else would be around to contradict the State case that the finder was also the killer. Moreover, a suspicion that the same person had an immoral association with the dead woman would, if spread widely enough by the killers, reach the ears of the Guards and be sufficient to make Gleeson a suspect. Careful planning, probably over a period of months, by the murderers, must have preceded Gleeson's arrest. Just how many people were in on this plan can only be guessed at now half a century or more later; but there had to be at least two able-bodied men, and probably three, involved. According to Dr. McGrath, Moll Carthy's white woollen pull-over had been pulled up under her arms. This, it is suggested, proved that she had been lifted and dragged (or carried) in a dead or dying condition. On the back of her coat Dr. McGrath had found mud, although there was none on the ground were she lay. This in turn shows that she had been dragged (or carried) along muddy ground or had been rested on muddy ground, possibly while those carrying her negotiated the ditch – the same ditch from which Gleeson said he noticed on the Thursday morning that some branches he had used a few days earlier to block the gap had been pushed aside. One of the police photographs shows what appears to be a fresh scar on one of Moll's legs, just as if the leg had been torn either by barbed wire or by a thorny bush.

If Moll Carthy was shot elsewhere than where she was found, no one person alone could have carried her body any distance. The almost total absence of blood anywhere in the vicinity of the spot where she lay (also testified to by Dr. McGrath) suggests that she had been carried some distance, possibly across two or three fields. Despite Mr. Justice Maguire's dogmatic dismissal of the idea, the theory that she was killed elsewhere and carried to the spot where she was found is, even on the State's evidence, much more convincing than the State case that she was killed where she was found. To carry her plump and heavily-clad body even across one field would obviously have required at least two strong men. Next, one must ask where she spent her last night alive, from 7.00 p.m. on Wednesday to 9.30 a.m. on Thursday. To this question there can, it is suggested, be only one answer: one or more of those who killed her (possibly the same man who had kept her out late on the Tuesday night) made an appointment to meet her on Wednesday night. Because of the cold weather it is, of course, unlikely that anyone would have risked bringing her to his home in all the circumstances. This pre-supposes the existence of some indoor meeting-place where Moll must have been held against her will, and where she probably got her last meal, of tea and bread as analysed by Dr. McGrath. As it happens, there was a disused and isolated dwelling-house, with a shed attached (both then in good repair, but now derelict), on land known as Lynch's farm, adjoining Caesar's land. These buildings would have ideally suited the killers' purposes, and are only three fields away from the spot where the body was found.

Having lured her to the empty buildings on Lynch's farm, her killers in all probability killed her there as dawn approached, with the first of the two shots fired at her. They then carried her body under cover of darkness to the spot where it was later found, where with their second shot they blew away her face, firing diagonally so as to ensure that traces of used shot from the cartridges became embedded in the adjoining ground, to give the impression that it was there that the murder had been committed. Because of the need to watch Gleeson's movements (which, as the next Chapter will show, continued right up to the Wednesday evening) in the weeks (perhaps months) before the murder, it seems likely that the number involved in the framing and in the murder itself had to be at least three. All in this group had to be local residents and close, even lifelong, friends, each trusted by the others in the view of the secrecy required. Today, over fifty years later, there are still people in New Inn who can identify the members of such an alleged group, who (unlike Harry Gleeson) had a motive for the murder. At least one of them is believed to have been involved in the simultaneous arson attacks in 1926 on the Carthy cottage and an adjoining vacant cottage.

By 1990 knowledge of my interest in the Gleeson affair had reached the ears of the then parish priest, Fr. James Meehan. Since his permission was required to inspect the school roll and other parish records, I told him the purpose of my research and informed him of my suspicions as to the identities of the real murderers, if Gleeson was innocent. Although not a native of the New Inn area, Fr. Meehan had spent much of his life there, first as a curate and later in the 1980s as its pastor. From many years' residence there he had won the confidence of the local people, in many of whose social activities he fully participated. Without informing me of his decision to do so, Fr. Meehan on his retirement embarked on his own private investigation into the Carthy murder, interviewing local families with knowledge or memories of the event – many of whom I did not (indeed, in a few cases, could not) approach. Because of his standing locally, he secured a degree of co-operation not normally accorded to outsiders. Not only that, but in several cases he was approached by local people who, for various prudent reasons, he had left out of his enquiries, as I had too. When his investigation was finished, he contacted me indirectly and had a message passed on to me that he had come to the conclusion that a group, such as I had earlier suggested, had in fact existed in 1940, and that one of them, whose identity was either volunteered to or confirmed by him by several local people, was the leader of the group. This man was the man whom Miss Cooney suspected of having fathered the last Carthy child, and bore the same surname as that deleted from my earlier account of Timoney's interview with a man who (with his wife) had once lodged with Moll Carthy. All concerned are now dead, including most recently Fr. Meehan himself.

One of the most controversial problems in the case is the part played by the Guards. Were they also set-up by the killers; or was any Guard in on the killers' plans? Because of the reputation locally of Guards Scully and Ruth, it seems that they (and probably the veteran Guard Gralton too) can be ruled out of any possible complicity in the framing of Gleeson. However, it is quite a different matter with Sergt. Daly; he was, after all, in charge of the inquiry locally. But there is more to it than just that. Within six months of his arrival in New Inn, from another Tipperary station nearby, he had become involved with Moll Carthy, compromising him in his official position. The visit he paid to her the afternoon she vanished has never been explained. The case for Daly's possible complicity begins with a story about him which still persists in New Inn. Some time after Gleeson's execution, while investigating a minor local crime, Daly approached a local man in a public-house to try to extract information from him to assist his enquiries. The man resented being used as a potential informant, and told Daly so. The conversation switched to the Gleeson case, still fresh in local memories. Suddenly Daly, now in an intoxicated condition, blurted out that on the night before Moll Carthy's body was found he had been told, by one of the men locally suspected of having planned the murder, that she had been killed.

I have spoken several times to the man approached in the public-house by Daly (the man still resides in Co. Tipperary), and I believe his account of the incident is truthful. If so, it suggests some link between Daly and those who framed Gleeson. It would explain why from the start police enquiries concentrated on Gleeson alone. It would also explain Daly's manner in the witness-box, when he gave the impression of a man who had something to hide. Any involvement by Daly with the killers would probably have been known to his colleagues in New Inn. This in turn would help to explain the readiness of Guards Ruth and Scully at the trial to disagree with Daly about Gleeson's first visit to the station and about the conversations with Gleeson that morning. It would also explain a tradition persisting in New Inn to this day that Guard Ruth always believed Gleeson to be innocent.

An accusation of complicity in a murder 53 years after the event, made against a police officer now dead, is so serious that an attempt has been made to be fair, both to the man and to the force. Enquiries in both Co. Tipperary and Daly's native county confirm that Anthony Daly was a highly efficient policeman. A member of the country's new police force almost from its foundation, he had carried out police duties during the War of Independence in a part of the country far from Tipperary, where such activities required exceptional courage. After almost 46 years' service in the new force he retired with what the records call an exemplary discharge. However, a question-mark must be placed over the number of transfers Daly got over a period of eighteen years – to Listowel in 1922, to Drumconrath in 1923, to Ardee in 1926, to Enfield in 1927, to Kiltegan in 1932, to Swanlinbar in 1936, to Bawnboy in 1936, to Ballingarry in 1940, and finally to New Inn the same year. Only once did he stay as long as five years in the same place; twice he was moved inside a year. In pre-1922 days such a record of rapid transfers usually suggested unsuitability for the post.

In Daly's native county I inspected a file of documents, relating to the War of Independence and compiled there by local historians in the 1960s. His record from 1918 to 1922 was outstanding. In an area where a substantial section of the population was hostile to the movement for independence, he displayed leadership of the highest order. However, two matters attracted attention. By some who know him he was regarded as untrustworthy, even unscrupulous. Moreover, when on his retirement he settled in a town in his native area, he neither re-built old friendships nor made any new ones. With his wife confined to hospital, he lived out a long and lonely retirement over a period of 23 years, in circumstances where one would have expected him to have enjoyed a pleasant sociable retirement.

If Sergt. Daly was in some way involved in the framing of Harry Gleeson, another question arises. To what extent was his superior officer,

Supt. Mahony, aware of this? There is, after all, some evidence to suggest that Mahony himself was unscrupulous, starting with his efforts to dissuade the Caesars from employing Timoney to defend Gleeson. There is also Mahony's admission to Mrs. Caesar that on 25 November his men had to beat information out of Thomas Reid. In the Summer of 1941, when discussing Reid's allegations of assault with Timoney, Mahony admitted that telegrams sent by the defence had been read in some unspecified telegraph office before delivery. This at once reminded Timoney of evidence he and Sean MacBride had uncovered around the same time of letters from Dublin to Timoney's Tipperary office having been tampered with, a matter neither of them had pursued at the time. Of all the Guards Timoney came into contact with when acting for Gleeson and Reid, including Daly, Mahony alone is the subject of adverse private comment in Timoney's file. Of course, the solicitor's view of the Supt. may have been influenced by the knowledge (assuming Gleeson had told him the truth) that, in all his meetings with Gleeson, Mahony had adopted a menacing or bullying attitude.

It is difficult to accept that all the improprieties (to use no stronger word) that seem to have occurred during the investigation of the murder went unnoticed by Supt. Mahony. These included the probable ill-treatment of Reid, the day-long virtual imprisonment in separate rooms at the local station of the Caesars, the tampering with the firearms register, the concealment from the defence of Fitzgerald's report of his shots at the cat, and the apparent doctoring of some important ballistics evidence, shortly to be explained. If Daly acted independently of his superintendent in any of these matters, he seems to have been confident that Mahony would either support him or at least turn a blind eye.

Four aspects of the case, not so far covered, may conveniently be mentioned here. The first concerns the references made in the District Court to a shortage of potatoes in the Carthy home on the week of the murder. Two of the three children gave evidence to this effect; neither repeated it at the trial. It is totally at variance with results of local enquiries, which suggest that potatoes (and bread too) were always available in abundance to Moll at the kitchen-door of Rockwell College. Secondly, and possibly connected with the suggestion of a scarcity of potatoes, is the prosecution evidence of the discovery in Carthy's house of a sack belonging to Caesar. What did not come out at the trial about this, and what might in any event not have been understood by the jury, is that because of the difference in texture of the meshes of the two types of sack in the pile, the Carthy boy could have picked out Caesar's beet-pulp sack had he been blindfolded. I understand from a member of the public, who was in court and has a farming background, that when Michael held up the sack it had so many holes that his fingers showed through it –

although Gleeson was supposed to have filled it with potatoes.

Thirdly, another puzzling aspect of Michael McCarthy's evidence in both courts concerned the trip he made on to Caesar's land on the Thursday morning. What was he doing up and out so early on a cold, damp November morning, something his neighbour Lenehan told the jury he never saw the boy do before except in Summer? Why did he hurry home the minute he saw Gleeson? Could it be because, as tests I have participated in suggest, from his vantage-point on the ditch which he climbed he could see his mother's body before Gleeson did? The mind boggles at the implications of this possibility. Finally one wonders why the older boy Patrick appears to have risen, dressed, eaten and left for work on the Thursday morning without any further apparent concern for his still missing mother. Could he not have made one further search of the fields, now that the rains had ceased and daylight returned?

Nor was this the end of possible police involvement. Research and tests carried out for this book point to the conclusion that not only was some of the ballistics evidence fudged by the Guards, but that more of it was false and misleading. Even to a person with no knowledge of firearms, some of the evidence of Supt. Daniel Stapleton, the State gun expert, appears questionable, if not actually unreliable. On relatively unimportant facts he admitted under cross-examination to at least three mistakes. He named the wrong Guard as the one who handed him one of the most important cartridges found in the vicinity of the body. He appeared to be unable to identify from the police location map which field was that known as the ploughed field, although it was marked as such. When reminded that a detective had sworn to having handed him a specific cartridge which the latter had only found a day earlier, Stapleton insisted that it was he himself who had found it. Cumulatively, these errors gave a general impression of unreliability by the most important State expert witness after the State Pathologist.

Regarding the manner in which Moll Carthy was shot in the neck (by the first of the two shots), the Supt. was positive that this had been fired from a horizontal position from a distance of only five or six feet. As a ballistics expert, Stapleton told the jury that his examination of the wound supported the prosecution case that the woman, when standing on one side of the fence, was shot by a person standing only feet away from her on the other side. As if to emphasise this expert opinion, Stapleton also swore that the second shot was fired from only six inches from her head or face and was fired downwards – "almost perpendicular". The total impression he conveyed of the actual moment of killing was of a person first shooting across the fence when both he and Moll were more or less level with each other and separated only by the fence, and of the killer then crossing the fence and firing a second shot downwards into the now fallen body. However, technical documentary evidence submitted by the defence engineer Munden, and not challenged, suggests something quite different. The section of the spot in question shows that the ground in the field where she was standing was fourteen inches lower than the ground in the Dug-Out Field on the far side of the fence. In addition, Moll Carthy only was five feet five inches in height, compared to Gleeson's five feet eleven inches. Accordingly, if he was the murderer, he had a total height advantage over her of twenty inches, so that it follows that Gleeson could not have fired the first shot horizontally at her; it would have had to have been fired diagonally downwards.

Nor are these the only grounds on which some of the vital ballistics evidence of Supt. Stapleton is open to challenge. Tests recently carried out, as well as expert advice obtained locally and from Britain – specifically from Eley Hawk in Birmingham, the makers of the cartridges in question, and from a firearms dealer in Co. Tipperary – throw a completely new light on Stapleton's evidence. They suggest the possibility that some of it was partly false or concocted. It is clear from his testimony that no identifying numbers or labels survived on any of the cartridges found by the Guards in or around the area where the body lay; if they had survived, Stapleton would have said so, as this would have lent his expert evidence more weight. In 1992 tests were carried out in New Inn, using ammunition from the 1940s identical to that used in Caesar's shot-gun. In nearly every such case the identification numbers or labels on such cartridges, fired from a gun similar to Caesar's, survived. It is difficult to understand why this did not happen also in Stapleton's tests; if it did, why did he not say so in court?

Copies of police photographs of the scene, taken shortly after the body was found and supplied to the defence, have all survived in mint condition in the MacBride Papers. They clearly show the copper end of one of the two cartridges which the State claimed were used to kill Moll Carthy facing upwards. However, recent tests in which dozens of 1940s cartridges were used established that the copper end of used and crumpled cartridges (which is the heavier end) never faces upwards, as in these photographs. The question to be asked: were those in the police photographs put there only for the photographs, and if so by whom and for what purpose, if not to mislead the judge and jury? In recent years, on or close to the exact anniversary of the murder of Moll Carthy, tests were carried out close to where she was found, to check the possibility of a person shooting with such accuracy as that sworn to by Supt. Reynolds regarding the first shot fired at Moll Carthy. These tests strongly pointed to the conclusion that a person standing at one side of fence at the time in question could not have fired accurately at Moll Carthy in the dark on the evening of 20 November 1940. At that time of the evening when the tests were carried out it was so dark that cattle grazing nearby could only be seen with difficulty. Supt. Stapleton also said he ascertained from weighing shot found on Caesar's land, and from shot extracted from the body, that the cartridges used by the killer were No. 5 shots, and many of his findings were based on this assumption. Yet, when Michael Leamy, the assistant in Feehan's hardware store in Cashel, expressed ignorance in court of whether Caesar had bought No. 4 or No. 5 cartridges, State counsel did not press the matter. If State counsel knew in advance what Stapleton would say, it would have been normal practice to tell the judge and jury during Leamy's evidence that it would later be proved that the shot was in fact No. 5. Why was this not done?

It is also possible that the Guards were to blame indirectly for the importance attached to the story told by Thomas Hennessy, the only person to hear two shots on the Wednesday – on whose evidence the whole State case for a Wednesday murder depended. Several reasons can be advanced for suggesting that he was not reliable. He claimed to have heard the shots from a spot that was three-quarters of a mile from where the body was found. Yet neither of two Carthy children, Michael and Mary, who were at home at the time and only a couple of fields away, heard them. Neither did Frank Lenehan, who told the jury he was out cycling then in the area, nor another neighbour of the Caesars, William Ryan, who was also out of doors walking a bicycle at the relevant time. The blacksmith John Ryan told Timoney that "if I was out when Hennessy heard the shots I would have heard them", adding "...but I am nearly sure I was in the house at the time". When later on the day of this interview Timoney met Ryan's brother Patrick, he said John had told him he had not reached home at the time Hennessy said he heard the shots: "If Hennessy heard them", John had told Patrick, "[I] ought to have...also".

The official weather reports of the time also discredit Hennessy's story. At 7.00 p.m. on Wednesday 20 November 1940 the wind direction at Foynes (the weather station on the Atlantic coast) was south-south-west, Force 1 Beaufort Scale. This supports the evidence which William Fitzgerald, who said the wind was from the south or south-west, gave in reply to the trial judge. Curiously, on the following day at the same time the wind direction was north-west and Force 3, a fact which explains why neither Reid nor Gleeson heard any shots on the Thursday morning, as such a wind would have carried the sounds away from them. Could it be that the information Hennessy gave the Guards related, not to the Wednesday evening, but to Thursday – the day, after all, that most New Inn people would have associated with the murder, because it was the day Moll Carthy's body was found? If Hennessy did hear shots on the Wednesday evening, what he heard was Fitzgerald shooting the cat in the tree – not with one shot (as Fitzgerald told Sergt. Daly), but with two shots (as Fitzgerald's employees first told Timoney before changing their stories).

At this stage one naturally becomes curious about Hennessy himself, to try to assess how reliable he might have been. Enquiries about him have produced the following information. In November 1940 he was 67 years of age, a bachelor living alone and with some eccentric habits for a man of his age, although to judge and jury he may have looked the essence of rural respectability. Also – and this is the police connection – he was assistant group leader of Section B of the Local Defence Force in New Inn, which worked closely with the local Guards.

If in fact Harry Gleeson was framed for the murder, the question has to be asked what motive had the real killers for the crime? There were, it is suggested, three possible motives, and it may have been that in the minds of the group responsible all three motives were inter-connected, or that each member of the group had a different motive. The first motive was simply the desire to rid the area of a woman whose life-style was disruptive of the local community. Secondly, just as Gleeson's solicitor discovered that Moll Carthy was employed in the local police station, one may assume that the group who planned her death also knew of this. For one or more of them the possibility that, even unwittingly, she was a source of useful information to the Guards would have provided sufficient reason to kill her, because at least one of the group is accepted locally as having been involved in subversive activities. The existence of an IRA cell only four miles away in the Rosegreen area was well known at the time; so was the fact that the area was the site of what is known in such circles as a safe house.

Given this factor, there were obvious dangers in Moll's employment by the Guards, especially as she had another type of involvement with one of the group, who had fathered at least one of her sons. That some of the Guards investigating Moll's murder were also engaged in anti-subversive activities is suggested by an incident involving Thomas Reid. On the morning of 27 November, two days after his day-long "visit" to New Inn police station, he found when he went to set off for the local creamery to deliver Caesar's milk that his ass had been apparently deliberately set loose and was missing. When he found the animal in a field nearby at a spot close to land owned by one of the group, he discovered that this man's house was under surveillance by a detective armed with a rifle. The detective made no attempt to conceal his presence, and even taunted Reid about the "straying" ass. It is suggested that no Guard, while on a murder hunt, would carry a rifle unless there was some paramilitary factor associated with the crime. One cannot rule out the possibility that the arrival at Moll's cottage, on both the Monday and the Wednesday of the previous week, of Guard Ruth and Sergeant Daly may have panicked the group into a decision to kill her. A meeting on the Wednesday night of the Local Security Force (the predecessor of today's F.C.A.) held in New Inn would have provided an alibi for at least one of the group.

Anybody who may have difficulty in understanding the fear, no matter now unfounded, of a police informer by a man involved in IRA activities in Co. Tipperary fifty years or so ago has only to look at the controversial Devereux affair of 1940-1942, much of the action in which took place not far from New Inn. In September 1940 Michael Devereux, a suspected IRA informer, disappeared near Grangemockler, some miles south-east of New Inn; a year later his body was found on nearby Slievenamon mountain. Three men were tried for his murder; two of them, George Plant and Patrick Davern, were from Co. Tipperary. Both were sentenced to death. Davern's sentence was commuted to life imprisonment, but Plant was executed by a firing squad. The Devereux affair was riddled with informers, from Stephen Hayes the IRA chief-of-staff who turned Government informer to James Crofton, a Guard who turned IRA informer. It is possible that, as the senior Guard locally, Sergt. Daly had a special role in anti-IRA activities. This would explain his transfer to New Inn in 1940 after only a few months in nearby Ballingarry. New Inn was closer to the known scene of IRA activities in Rosegreen, where some of those suspected of involvement in the Devereux killing were reputed to be in hiding.

The third possible motive for the Carthy murder, although a personal one, is no less likely for that reason. As already mentioned, one of the group believed to have been responsible had fathered at least one of the Carthy boys. This man may have become increasingly concerned as Moll came more and more to defy the local community; and he may have made a discovery that gave him grounds for this concern. Although the births of all her seven children were registered with the father's name unspecified, examination of the local parish register reveals a curious fact. By her choice of first name for at least five of the children, she clearly signalled the father's identity. As the clerk of the church at the time was not one to keep such secrets to himself, one may assume Moll's use of this device became known locally, and got to the ears of at least some of the fathers. It was, incidentally, from this same church official that Thomas Reid learned of the birth, death and burial of the last Carthy child, he later told Timoney.

Chapter 9

Tommy Reid gives Harry an alibi

On a warm afternoon in early Autumn of 1992 I was driven from Co. Tipperary across the county boundary into a neighbouring county, where we pulled up in a tiny remote single-street village. We had come by appointment to meet Tommy Reid, Harry Gleeson's fellow-employee on Caesar's farm in 1940. Long since retired, Reid had recently been visited by a couple of men from Co. Tipperary and had agreed to meet me. The front door of a small terraced house opened, to reveal a low-sized spare figure with sprinkled grey hair, who shook hands firmly if a little shyly. Once all three of us were inside his spotless living-room he made tea, and we sat around the open fire he had obviously lit for his visitors. As he seemed a little ill at ease, I tried to gain his confidence by asking how he had spent the 51 years since Harry's death. He had left New Inn afterwards for good, cutting all links with the place where he had grown to manhood, been treated by the Caesars as one of the family and accepted by the neighbours. He had moved to Dublin, where for years he had worked for a steel firm, until the physical work became too much for him. A lifelong bachelor, he had settled in this secluded spot less than an hour's car-drive from New Inn.

Gradually Tommy Reid's manner became more relaxed. He did not look anywhere near his mid-seventies, and moved agilely round the room as he served tea and built up the fire. Mentally too he seemed years younger than his real age, showing a good memory of people and places he had not seen for decades and displaying a quick sense of humour as he heard news of old friends in Co. Tipperary. The conversation turned to his assault case against the two police officers who, he still insisted, had ill-treated him in the local station. He had spent the whole day there, he recalled, while Caesar's ass stood tethered to the rail outside; unknown to him, the two Caesars waited all day in separate rooms from each other in the same building. His tone grew quieter but more serious as he told how his neighbours next day commented on the marks on his face. I told him I had seen the long statement his solicitor had taken from him a few days later. Privately I marvelled as I heard Reid repeat some of the words and phrases which John Timoney, himself now long dead, had taken down in longhand 52 years before. A slight note of bitterness became evident as he told how he lost the case. But he said his lawyers had done a good job, specially Mr. Lavery, who later became a Supreme Court judge. As he saw Guard after Guard (all, he thought, in uniform except the Chief Superintendent), go into the box and deny any assault, he knew he hadn't a chance.

After what seemed an age to me, we got Reid round to the Gleeson case. After some general remarks during which I wondered if he would continue at all, we got him to concentrate on the Wednesday afternoon, 20 November – 52 years earlier, give or take a few weeks. Speaking quietly but firmly, Reid said he had been out milking the cows in a field adjoining the lane running from the road to Caesar's yard. It was dusk as he finished, and as he entered the lane from the field he rested the two pails full of fresh milk on the ground to shut the gate. Suddenly he realised in the oncoming darkness that someone was watching him from the mouth of the lane. The figure withdrew behind the now thinning hedge, but Reid recognised him by his riding breeches. This man had been wearing them for some months, Reid remarked, but never wore them again after that evening. Picking up his two pails, Reid walked up the lane into the farmyard. When he had put away the milk, he went to a tank in the yard to rinse his hands. Harry was standing beside him now; he had come in from ploughing, Reid said. I asked Reid what time this was. He was not sure – "between 6.30 and 7.00, probably nearer to 7.00." Suddenly in the dark two shots rang out as Harry, who had just washed a dog-pan at the tank, turned to go into the house for supper. "By God, Harry, whoever fired those shots must have cats' eyes", Reid remarked. Gleeson, his back to Reid, said nothing. Later Reid wondered if Gleeson, who (he now reminded us) was "a bit deaf", had heard him at all. The shots, Reid said, sounded very far off. Privately I wondered if these were Fitzgerald's shots at the cat, as the wind was from that direction.

There was silence now in Reid's living-room as he finished, almost as if he realised the impact what he had just told us had made. Before I could get a word in, the man who had driven me over from Tipperary leaned across and quietly asked: "But Tommy, didn't you ever tell this to anyone?" Without hesitation Reid replied, "I did", and then went on. The following morning, after Harry returned from the barracks and the Guards (all but Guard Ruth, still down at the Dug-Out) had left, Mrs. Caesar called in both Gleeson and himself and questioned them about where they were the previous evening. Once she heard Reid's account of the shots she issued her orders, as she always did in that house. Since both were in the clear, they were to say nothing to the Guards, and keep completely away from them too. Reid, the younger of the two – only 25 to Gleeson's 37 – obeyed her to the word, even when under oath, with literally fatal results for Gleeson.

As Reid finished, a hitherto cryptic comment by Sean MacBride, in an interview 35 years after the Carthy murder, became clear to me. "He [Gleeson]...didn't commit the crime because he couldn't have committed it as...he was elsewhere at the time", MacBride said in 1974 to the journalist Vincent Browne, now editor of the *Sunday Tribune*. Whether or not the two shots Reid heard with Gleeson standing beside him were, in fact, those that killed Moll Carthy was irrelevant, as MacBride must have realised whenever he later heard Reid's story. What mattered was that, had the jury heard Reid's story and believed it, the State case would have collapsed. What convinced me that Reid in his home last year told me the truth is another revelation he made the same day, which was to Gleeson's discredit. As we resumed discussion of the case, one of us asked him if he believed Harry really did not recognise the body when he first saw it. To our astonishment, Reid replied (without hesitation again) that the moment Gleeson saw it he had in fact realised it was Moll, and also that she was dead. On reflection, that Reid was telling the truth is also confirmed by the failure of the Caesars to send him out to identify the body while Gleeson was gone to New Inn. If Gleeson had not recognised the body and said so to his uncle and aunt, Mrs. Caesar would at once have dispatched Reid to where the body lay before the Guards arrived, to see if he recognised it.

With hindsight it is easy now to appreciate the dilemma Gleeson found himself in, when he looked over the fence that morning and saw Moll's mutilated body on the other side. There on his uncle's land early in the morning, when he knew he was the first person to be out, lay the body of this local woman, "with her previous pedigree" to use her neighbour's cruel phrase; a woman Harry could not deny knowing, as her property adjoined his uncle's farm; a woman whose straying goats had caused trouble for him and Reid down the years, and had even led to unpleasantness between them. Nor can his single falsehood, made for all one now knows under pressure from uncle or aunt, be used to argue for Gleeson's guilt, on the basis that if he told one lie how could one believe anything else he said. One has only to read his two statements, specially the longer one taken under police caution on 25 November, to sense that they were consistent with each other and were the words of a person with nothing to hide. (See Appendix I). If, after all, Gleeson was innocent, he knew from an early stage that he had nothing to lose by describing every movement of his over the previous week or so, which is precisely what he insisted on doing in his longer statement.

In a draft of a closing speech for the defence, written in Sean

MacBride's hand and found among his papers, he suggested that "Mary McCarthy was a victim of a perverted sense of morality bred by a civilisation which, nominally based on Christianity, lacks most of [its] essentials." One might add that, through the conspiracy of silence which prevented Harry Gleeson's lawyers from mounting an adequate defence on his behalf, that same perversion made him a second victim of the unchristian civilisation. For MacBride and Timoney, both comparatively inexperienced lawyers still in their thirties, the Gleeson case was an experience neither ever forgot. To MacBride it showed the awful risk of a miscarriage of justice where the penalty was death. It led him directly to campaign vigorously for the abolition of capital punishment, something he lived to see achieved many years later after he had had a successful public and international career. For Timoney, who came from a politically conservative background, it brought him under the spell of the older man and into the Dail for a brief period in the late 1940s, with MacBride as his leader.

For the rest of their lives the two men never ceased to discuss the fate of Harry Gleeson, from time to time collecting new bits of information that gradually enabled them to fit the pieces of this bizarre legal jig-saw into place. In September 1943, over two years after Gleeson's hanging, they were still exchanging volumes of the transcript of evidence, which only then they had found time to read at leisure. Convinced that the firearms register held vital clues to the case, Timoney, in an effort to get a sight of the book, boldly walked into Feehan's shop in Cashel in July 1941, and for the only time in his life bought a box of cartridges. By then his professional file on the Gleeson case was closed, and Feehan himself (whom he presumably met on that occasion) is dead. So whether or not this particular mission succeeded cannot be said. With Sean MacBride too the case remained an abiding passion. Two of his private secretaries in turn have told me that he never stopped talking and thinking about it. On frequent visits to Tipperary, where he had some close friends, he would tease out angles of the case that still puzzled him. In the early 1980s he spoke to a younger generation of champions of Gleeson's innocence, as convinced as their elders that Harry was hanged in the wrong. Today, with all connected with the murder dead, there is a greater readiness to discuss it, and even among some at least a feeling that the law got the wrong man. Yet even in the Tipperary of the 1990s one cannot say with certainty that all traces of the conspiracy of silence are gone for good.

Many years after the Gleeson case, the distinguished actor, Cyril Cusack, visited Tipperary professionally, and John Timoney and his wife gave a party for him at their home in the town. Late into the night the visitor asked Timoney what had been his most memorable case. Timoney at once began to tell the story of Harry Gleeson, the case that still refuses to go away 53 years later. He unfolded the tale of intrigue and silence that he and Seán MacBride had by then almost fully pieced together. As he recalled MacBride's last visit to the condemned man only hours before he mounted the scaffold, still insisting after making his peace with his God that he was innocent, and pleading with his lawyer to clear his good name, John Timoney broke down. To try to clear the good name of Harry Gleeson has been the sole reason for writing this book.

Appendix I

EXHIBIT 10

STATEMENT OF HENRY GLEESON, TAKEN AT THE DWELLING HOUSE OF JOHN CAESAR, AT MARLHILL, NEW INN, CO TIPP. AT 12.10 p.m. ON MONDAY, 25th NOVEMBER, 1940, AFTER THE SAID HARRY GLEESON HAD BEEN CAUTIONED BY SUPERINTENDENT P. MAHONY, that he was not obliged to say anything unless he wished to do so and that anything he might say would be taken down in writing and might be used in evidence.

"I am about 38 years. I was born in Galbertstown, Holycross. I know that I have been cautioned by Supt. Mahony, that I am not obliged to say anything unless I wish to do so, and that anything I do say will be taken down in writing and may be used in evidence."

"I have been living with my uncle John Caesar for the past 16 years. When I came to live with him first he was residing at Graigue, New Inn, about half a mile from here. He sold a farm he had at Graigue about 13 years ago, when he purchased this place. My uncle John was married twice. His first wife was alive when I came to live with him. She died a short time before he sold his farm at Graigue. He married his present wife the Shrove after he buying the place at Marlhill where he now resides."

"I am not paid a wage by my uncle, but any time I want a pound or three pounds or more I have it to get from my uncle or his wife. I have got no promise from my uncle that I will get his farm at any time. The way things are, if my uncle and his Mrs. were gone I believe I would have the best right to the farm and that if I did not get it I would get a fair thing out of it. I have been on excellent terms with my uncle's wife since they were married, just as if she were my mother. I never had a row with my uncle or his wife but if I was out late my uncle might say something to me but I knew it would be for my good. I drink stout but I was never drunk except maybe once."

QUESTIONED BY SUPERINTENDENT:

QUESTION	Give the names of all the people who live in the house.
ANSWER	Myself, my uncle, my aunt and Thomas Reid.
QUESTION	Where do each of you sleep?
ANSWER	I sleep mostly over the sitting room. Thomas Reid sleeps

	over the kitchen and my uncle and aunt sleep in the room off the kitchen opposite the fire. I have now looked at the rooms and I know that I sleep over the kitchen and not over the sitting room.
QUESTION	Where does Reid sleep?
ANSWER	In the summer time he sleeps on the loft in the barn and in the winter time he comes inside and sleeps in the bedroom over the kitchen next to my bedroom. He is sleeping in the bedroom over the kitchen since last Monday night – this night week.
QUESTION	Have yourself and your uncle and aunt always slept in the same rooms since you came here?
ANSWER	Always in the same rooms.
QUESTION	Are there any other bedrooms in the house?
ANSWER	There are two other rooms which my aunt keeps locked for visitors, and they are over the sitting-room.
QUESTION	Has the question of your marriage ever been considered between yourself and your uncle and aunt?
ANSWER	Of all the things out it never troubles me. My uncle was often twarting us about it. My aunt has a niece who comes here on holidays sometimes and when my uncle would come in from town he would tell her to grow up and get strong and the two of us could be married – meaning I and she.
QUESTION	What age is your aunt's niece?
ANSWER	She is about 14 years.
QUESTION	What is her name? What is her address?
ANSWER	[Name deleted].
QUESTION	Did you hand over all your clothes to us this morning?
ANSWER	All the clothes except my Sunday boots.
QUESTION	About the dirty shirt that you handed over, during what period did you wear that?
ANSWER	I took it off yesterday morning and put on the clean one that is gone away. I usually change my shirt every Sunday except in wet weather when the Mrs. couldn't get them dry. I may have that dirty one on more than a week. I had it on at the last fair of Cashel anyway.
QUESTION	Do you wish to say anything about the stain which is around the neck of that dirty shirt?
ANSWER	I had it on the last fair of Cashel. I was at the fair. The day was very wet. The rain ran down my neck shoulders and back from my cap and head and wet it. When I was going to bed on the fair night I took off the shirt and brought it

	down, and hung it over the fire in the kitchen on the crane, and it may have got scorched, sir.
QUESTION	Who washes the clothes of the house?
ANSWER	The Mrs. generally for the last three months. She has only to wash for myself, the boss and herself. Reid does his own laundry; he is as good as a girl.
QUESTION	Did your aunt ever get any help to wash the clothes?
ANSWER	She used to get a little woman named Nan Brennan of Cahir to help her, up to about twelve months ago. She (Brennan) used bowl in off the bus and if my aunt had any heavy washing she would get her to do it and she would scuttle off then in the evening. During the past summer the Mrs. used to give Mrs. Tommy Ryan of Tullamaine, New Inn, table cloths to get washed in some laundry. In my time I never saw anybody else washing laundry there.
QUESTION	Will you tell us as well as you can remember what you were doing all last week commencing with Monday last – this day week?
ANSWER	I'll tell you. Start with Saturday when I was cutting the grass. I likely got up at the usual time. Tommy Reid and myself had our first breakfast before we went out. I went to the field to milk the cows. Tommy Reid prepared the ass and box for the creamery and followed me to the field with them. We milked the cows, then Tommy went on to the creamery and I came back with the buckets and some milk for the day. After that I took out the hounds for the usual walk up through the cattle. When I came back with the hounds I put them in and fed them. When that was done the boss and Mrs. were at their breakfast and I joined them. After the breakfast I said to the boss I would go ploughing and to go and mark out the field for me. That is the field marked No. 7 on the map. While he was doing that I helped the Mrs. with some jobs around the house. It would be about 11 o'clock a.m., old time, when I got to the field with the horses and plough. My uncle was still there marking out the field. I only spent about an hour ploughing because the day got misty. I came home and the Mrs. and boss were then preparing to go to Cashel. Tommy Reid was doing kitchen work when I came in. It was he got the dinner. After the dinner I said to Reid "make the cup of tea for me now and I will go cleaning the ditch then." I took up the slasher to the field where I was ploughing and cut the briars and grass at the headland

where I used to turn the horses. When I had the grass and briars cut, I cut some overhanging boughs off the big bush that is near the dug-out. When I had the boughs cut I put them together with the slasher and put them up in the gap near the bush. I put no sod or anything over them. Then I gathered together the grass and briars also and put them in little heaps at the butt of the ditch. I came home and then stayed around the yard while Tommy Reid was milking the cows. When Tommy came back I took out the hounds and went up as far as the hill field, No. 5 on map. I went up to see the cattle and to see if the bull was staying peacefully with them. I came back down the same way, back to No. 2 field. I crossed over then to Ned Lynch's land and all through Ned Lynch's land until I went out on the road at John Leamy's, for I had money to give Leamy, for my seat in a car which took us to Kilfeacle last Wednesday week to a coursing meeting. Myself and John Leamy were talking on the road beyond about the Kilfeacle coursing. After talking for about five or ten minutes with John Leamy I came home around the road with Stephen Barrett, Marlhill. I met Barrett at Leamy's. After parting with Barrett at his home I came in home along the boreen. When I landed in here I put up my hounds and fed them. I took my supper then and started reading the papers the boss and Mrs. brought from town. I was reading for about an hour. I then went and let out the animals I was working with earlier in the day, and the pony my uncle and aunt had in the town. When I had all that done and all the gates and things secured I came in and read the paper until I went to bed at about 9.00 p.m. old time.

Sunday morning we were up a bit earlier than usual. I lit the fire and put on the kettle, prepared breakfast for myself and Thomas Reid. After the breakfast Tommy Reid went off milking. I let the animals in out of the field. The two horses and the pony, I fed them, and prepared myself for first Mass in New Inn. I went to Mass. When Mass was over I came home immediately. When I came in here the boss said the bull was gone – that there was no account of him. I took my breakfast, put on my old clothes, let out my hounds and went in search of the bull. I got the bull in Paddy Burn's farm with Paddy Burn's cattle. I got him back and put him in to a house, came into my dinner. When I had my dinner taken I brought two of my hounds up to

Dogstown. Myself, Pat Coman, Mick Maloney, Mick Leamy and John Leamy gave all day hunting at Dogstown. It was dark when I returned home. I done my usual feeding of the hounds; took my supper and got my bicycle and went up to Mike Barron's of Belleview. Hold on now, he was with us too at Dogstown on Sunday. Oh God, no I am wrong, he was in Kilfeacle that day. I stayed at Belleview until about 10.30 p.m. old time, talking about the trials in Kilfeacle. I then came home and went to bed. Monday morning I was up some time after seven old time; lit the fire and made the breakfast for myself and Tommy Reid. After the breakfast I went to milk the cows. Tommy Reid prepared the ass and followed me over. When we had the cows milked Tommy Reid went to the creamery and I brought back the two buckets. I let in the horses; fed them and let in the pony too; let out my hounds and did my usual herding. When I had that done I came back down and fed my hounds; took my breakfast; done a few little jobs with the Mrs. and went off to the garden ploughing. That was the same garden that I was ploughing in on Saturday. When I came back to my dinner the boss was gone to Cashel. When I had my dinner taken I went ploughing again until about half four or a quarter to five, p.m. old time. I then brought in my horses, fed them, took out my hounds, done my usual runs through the fields with them, brought them in and fed them; took my supper and got the daily paper. I was reading the daily paper until about 8 o'clock p.m. old time. I let out the horses then and the pony and came in to the fire when I had all closed up outside; took off my boots and stayed at the fire for about a quarter of an hour or 20 minutes talking to the boss and Mrs. before I retired to bed. Tuesday morning I got up; lit the fire; got the breakfast for myself and Tommy Reid; got a bucket each and went to the cows. I had the horses in before we went to the cows. When we came back from milking Tommy Reid done the jobs around the house that I used to do when he would be gone to the creamery. I let out my hounds; travelled all the fields through the cattle and through the sheep; came in; put up my hounds; fed them; took my breakfast and went to the garden ploughing. I came in to my dinner; put up my horses first and fed them; took my own dinner. By the time we finished our dinner Michael Cantwell and Bouchy Kane arrived into the yard in a motor car. They bought four fat pigs off the boss. "Well then," the boss says to me, "what way will we get them in." So Michael Cantwell said he was going to Cahir to see about a lorry and that if he got the lorry he would come back again to let us know. So Michael Cantwell left the yard. I came into the kitchen and the Mrs. said "Blow the fire until I make a sup of tea for you before you go to the garden." I says to the Mrs. "I'll go over to the pump in the field where we milk the cows to see are there water in the pots and things." On I leaving the yard Mrs. Tommy Ryan and the daughter came into the yard in a motor car. I went on out the boreen in the cow gate, into the field which is marked 15 on the map. I went from that field into the paddock where the pump is. The pump field is marked No. 11a on the map. I went down straight to the pump; filled the pots. Coming back up the same route I stood at the gate between field Numbers 11a and 15 and looked around. I saw Moll Carthy quite convenient to her house, spancelling goats. I continued on to the boreen and back to my uncle's house.

QUESTION   What hour of the day was it when you were at the pump?
ANSWER   I'll say between 1.00 and half-one old time after dinner.
QUESTION   Were you long at the pump?
ANSWER   About five minutes. When I returned to the house I came into the kitchen. The teapot was at the fire. My aunt Mrs. Tommy Ryan and Tommy Ryan's eldest daughter were at the fire. I took my tea, pulled out the horses and went ploughing. The same evening came very wet about four o'clock old time so I had to come in out of the garden and I put up the horses and came in and sat down at the fire talking to Mrs. Tommy Ryan. It cleared off after about a quarter of an hour. I went out in the barn. The boss was there fixing a trough. I says to him "I'll bring up the slasher to the gap where the bull broke out." He agreed. I went up to the gap; cut bushes and fenced it. Well, at the time I was at the gap it would be about 5 o'clock old time p.m. So I had only a couple of forks of bushes cut before it was dark. I came down into the yard with the slasher and fork; put them into the barn. The boss said "don't mind the horses. I am after feeding them." So I came into my supper. When I had my supper finished it would be in or about a quarter after six p.m. old time. I took out my hound, only one hound, that's the hound I am making up

for Clogheen; went into the boreen and up the Marlhill road over as far as about twenty or thirty yards beyond Martin Donnell's. I was going to go as far as the village for a paper as we had no paper because there was no creamery but I changed my mind and turned back as the night was looking bad. I continued my journey back until I came to John Halpin's. I went into John Halpin's kitchen door to know had he the daily paper read. Mrs. Halpin came to the door to me and she wanted me in and I said "I can't go in. I have a hound but would she have the daily paper read." She said I think I am after burning it. John Halpin spoke and said "maybe it is yesterday's paper you burned." So John got up and got the paper I wanted. He handed me the paper at the door. I was in the yard the whole time. I thanked him and returned home; put in my hound and fed the three hounds; came in with the paper. The Mrs. and boss were at the fire. I opened the paper and took out the sports side of it, that's where the coursing and dogs do be. The Mrs. and boss took up the rest of it – parts each of it. So when I was satisfied with the bit I had I got the flash lamp, and went out to let out the horses. I let out the horses; shut up all the gates and doors and came in; took off my boots and got another part of the paper which my uncle or aunt had finished with. So I retired to bed about nine o'clock p.m., old time. We were up early on Wednesday morning. It could be before 7, sir, for the lorry was to be here for the pigs at 9 o'clock, a.m., new time. I lit the fire the same as usual and made the breakfast for myself and Tommy Reid. I let the horses into the house and fed them. Myself and Tommy Reid went over the boreen to the cows; brought back the two buckets of milk; put them into the dairy and I went over and let out the three hounds. I went up to look at the cattle. The cattle were in the second field from the house which is number 3 on map. I went from the second field out the iron gate into the dug-out field. We had lambs there. I went through them and down to the iron gate leading into the partly ploughed field to see the other sheep. So when I had them seen I returned home; put in my hounds and fed them, and came into my breakfast. It would be about 9 o'clock, a.m., old time, then. The lorry had not yet arrived for the pigs. So we stayed around the yard expecting the lorry every minute. I was tired from being around the yard. I got a shovel and cleaning old briars and things along our turnip garden ditch. So Michael Cantwell arrived out in a motor car while I was at the ditch in the boreen, so he stopped and he asked me did the lorry come. I says "not yet." So the word Michael said then was "what am I going to do to get them in." I said to him "go in and see the boss." I followed him in. I brought in the slasher and shovel. So when I arrived in the yard the boss says "Go out to John Halpin and get the jennet and waggon." I sat into the car with Michael Cantwell and went out to Halpin's house. John was just in from the creamery. I asked him and he told me I could get the jennet and waggon. So, John went to catch the old jennet for me and I went preparing the waggon; in the meantime the lorry arrived and stopped to know where the house was from John Halpin. When I saw the lorry stopping I went down and I sat in the lorry and we came on to the house for the pigs. So when the pigs were loaded the boss went off in the lorry to Cashel with the pigs. The Mrs., Tommy Reid and myself had our dinner. When we had our dinner taken the Mrs. got ready to go to the town, that's to Cashel – to bring home the boss. When the Mrs. was gone I prepared the animals for to go ploughing. Tommy Reid made tea for myself and himself and when I had it taken I went ploughing. I was ploughing until about four o'clock, p.m. old time. It would be in or about 2.00 p.m. old time, when I went ploughing. After yoking in the horses to plough at 2.00 p.m. and before I started to plough I went down along the headland and got out over the broken down gap for to relieve a lamb which was caught in briars in the dug-out field. The lamb was caught in briars at the fence which divides the dug-out field from the partly ploughed field. I could not say what length the lamb was from the dug-out corner. I saw the lamb entangled when I was coming out with the horses. When I had the lamb relieved I came back the same way by the broken down gap at the dug-out and started off with the horses ploughing. When I finished ploughing I brought in my horses in order to let Tommy Reid go milking. Tommy Reid was around the house while the Mrs. and boss were in town until I returned from ploughing. Tommy Reid went off milking immediately after I coming in from the garden where I was ploughing. That would be about a quarter after four old time, p.m. when he went milking. I was feeding the horses and other little jobs when the boss and Mrs. arrived in from town at about half-past four old time, p.m. I took the pony from him and put him up to and fed him; put in the messages out of the car; put the car in the barn and came into the kitchen. The Mrs. asked me to do something and I made a remark that I would take out the hounds while I had light. I let out the hounds, went into No. 1 field through a small gate into No. 4 field; from No. 4 field into No. 6 field; and from No. 6 field, in the iron gate, to No. 7 field which is partly ploughed, down along the headland where there is a tar tin and out over a broken-down gap where there are sticks across into No. 11 field; across that field into No. 11a field – the pump field; out the wooden gate of that field into No. 15 field; out into the boreen then and home along the boreen. When I came home I put in my hounds and fed them and came into my supper. While I was at my supper, the Mrs., the boss, myself and Tommy Reid were at our supper together. I asked the boss did he hear in Cashel what won in Kilsheelan. So he says "there is a paper in my topcoat pocket at the staircase." When I had my supper taken I got the paper out of his pocket. It was the Independent. I pulled the chair under the lamp and started reading the paper. That would be in or about 6 o'clock p.m. old time. I was at the paper for about half an hour, or it might be a little more, when Willie Ryan, Mrs. Fitzgerald's working man, came in. Myself and Willie Ryan, the boss and the Mrs. were around the fire. The boss was twarting him over the Mortellstown social dance which was held in New Inn. The boss said he heard he was dancing with a foxy girl from Cashel. I was enquiring who was at the dance and we had a discussion about it and also about running. We had no other conversation. About 8 o'clock p.m. old time, I stood up; got the flash lamp and walked out to let out the horses and the pony. I let them out and secured all the gates and doors. I walked in and put up the lamp; took off my boots and stayed at the fire with Willie Ryan, the boss and Mrs. and went to bed about half eight p.m. old time. I don't know what time Willie Ryan left, or what time the boss and Mrs. went to bed. Let them account for themselves. Thursday morning we were up at the usual time; I lit the fire, made the breakfast for myself and Tommy Reid. When we had the breakfast taken I let in the horses into the house; fed them and went off milking with Tommy Reid over the boreen. We had a bucket each, and when going over I asked him did he hear in the village what won the Tipperary coursing cup at Kilsheelan. He was able to tell me all the locals were knocked out. When we had the cows milked we were back again into the yard together. We put the milk into the dairy and after doing that I noticed that the bull was gone from the four cattle which were in the middle field, which is No. 3 field on map. I walked over across and let out one hound which I am making up for Clogheen coursing. I put the lead on him until I got out to No. 2 field on the map. I let him loose then and walked straight up to the gap where the bull broke out on Sunday. That gap is on the fence which bounds our land and Bill Gorman's and in the hill field as shown on map. The bull was in our field and at the gap. He was looking into Gorman's field through the bushes which fence the gap. When he saw me he doubled away from the gap. I hadn't to follow him as he returned to our own cattle himself. The hound did not follow. He stayed with me all the time. He would not follow cattle or sheep although he would follow a rabbit alright. I then crossed a broken-down gap from the hill field to the dug-out field and down towards the dug-out by the boundary fence, making my way to see ewes which were in the partly ploughed field – which is numbered 7 on the map. Before I came to the dug-out gap I caught up my dog. He was playing with an old cattle skull which was in the dug-out field. I put the dog on the lead.

QUESTION	Why did you put him on the lead at this particular place?
ANSWER	It was easy to catch him when he was playing with the old

skull. I did not want him to be loose going through the sheep. Having the dog on the lead I went for the gap to go out in the partly ploughed field where the ewes are. I was mostly up on the gap when little black dog growled at me. I looked out and I saw that there was a woman with the little dog so I turned back off the ditch and came into the house; put my hound into his house and went into the bedroom door where my uncle and aunt sleep. I told them "There is a woman and a little dog in the corner of the field where I was ploughing." They asked me where and I said "outside the dug-out." I says "wouldn't it be better see the Guards." I don't know what my uncle and aunt said as

	I scuttled off to the barracks at New Inn.
QUESTION	You have not described the position of the woman or the dog.
ANSWER	In my opinion they were in the same position as they were when the sergeant and Grd. Ruth came on the scene.
QUESTION	Did you make any effort to find out if anything was wrong with the woman when you first saw her?
ANSWER	No.
QUESTION	Did you know the woman or the dog?
ANSWER	No. I didn't know either.
QUESTION	You knew Mary McCarthy when you saw her 250 yards away on Tuesday; how is it you did not know her when you stood over her on Thursday?
ANSWER	I didn't wait to know who was in it.
QUESTION	Did you not know the dog?
ANSWER	I did not know the dog, for I used to have no recourse to that place in the evenings, and you would not see a sinner stirring there in the morning.
QUESTION	When you arrived at the fence where you saw the woman lying what impression did you get of her?
ANSWER	My impression was that she was lying there – that she could be either sleeping or dead.
QUESTION	Why did you report at the Guards' barracks that she was dead?
ANSWER	I mentioned sleeping as well as dead to Guard Scully.
QUESTION	Did you notice anything wrong with the woman's head that morning?
ANSWER	No. It is by her petticoats I knew she was a woman. Her knees were partly stripped.
QUESTION	Where was the dog when you first saw him?
ANSWER	He was lying on her breast with his tail to her knees.
QUESTION	What position was the dog in when you arrived with the Guards?
ANSWER	He was in the same position as when I first saw him.
QUESTION	When did you first recognise the woman?
ANSWER	When myself and Sergt. Daly and Grd. Ruth arrived on the spot Sergt. Daly said "it is Molly Carthy." I said "God, it must be, look at the foxy head."
QUESTION	Did any of you know the dog?
ANSWER	The sergeant asked me at the barracks what kind the dog was and I said a little black pom. Sometime later, either on the road from the barracks to where the body lay, at the spot or on the return journey to the house I told the

118

	sergeant that I used see a little white dog with the McCarthy's but I never saw the black one with them.
QUESTION	When did you last see the little white dog at McCarthy's?
ANSWER	About three weeks or a month ago I saw a little white dog lying on the dyke by their yard gate. I had often seen the same dog before that around their field but I never saw a dog at McCarthy's like the one I saw at the body.
QUESTION	Who brought the dog from the body to Caesar's house?
ANSWER	I did.
QUESTION	How did you hold him?
ANSWER	I caught him by the back of the neck and held him at my arm's length in my right hand. I don't think I changed him from one hand to the other because he was light.
QUESTION	What age is your uncle?
ANSWER	I suppose he is in or around seventy.
QUESTION	When he came home from Cashel on last Wednesday evening was he sober?
ANSWER	He was. He may have a couple of drinks taken but he was sober and knew what he was about.
QUESTION	How long have you known Molly McCarthy?
ANSWER	I have known her since I came to this side of the country from my own home. That is about 16 years, but I had not much recourse with her until we came to live here about 13 or 14 years ago.
QUESTION	Did she ever work here?
ANSWER	Not since we came here.
QUESTION	Will you give us an idea of what dealing you had with her since you came to live here?
ANSWER	I will. We often cut trees on the side of the road near where she lived and I used tell her she could have the light branches. The same thing happened when we cut furze or bushes off the ditches. She often took branches or bushes without any permission. She often got water in the pump in field numbered 11a on map, and also in the pump at the house. That was happening generally since we came in here. She always had a flock of goats and they used trespass on my uncle's land. She used be after them. I met her frequently when she was taking away bushes; drawing water; or turning out the goats. I was always friendly with her and spoke to her often – always when I met her. I often cautioned her about the goats trespassing, and a month or two ago our boy – Tommy Reid – was flogging the goats out of our field. Michael saw him and threatened

119

	the Guards on him, and said "give us back the traps you stole from us."
QUESTION	How do you know what happened between Tommy Reid and Michael McCarthy?
ANSWER	Tommy Reid told me the evening it happened.
QUESTION	Did you ever give potatoes to Molly McCarthy unknown to your uncle?
ANSWER	I did. About two years ago I gave her a butt of potatoes. I took them over in the ass and box and threw them in over her fence about dusk one evening. My aunt or uncle knew nothing about that.
QUESTION	Did anybody else know anything about it?
ANSWER	No. I often gave her son – Sonny – apples because he used to pump water for us at the pump in the field, No. 11a, for the cattle when we used to be busy. He gave me live rabbits two or three times last April and I paid him for them. He asked me later if I wanted any more rabbits and I said no that they were too slow.
QUESTION	When you were down at the pump last Tuesday were you talking to Moll Carthy?
ANSWER	No, sir.
QUESTION	Did you get a bag from her that day to get potatoes for the next day, while your uncle would be away?
ANSWER	No.
QUESTION	When you were at the pump did you know that your uncle would be away the following day with the pigs?
ANSWER	I did.
QUESTION	Did you make an appointment with Molly Carthy that day (Tuesday last) to meet her on Wednesday evening with the potatoes near the dug-out?
ANSWER	No, sir.
QUESTION	Did you ever at any time take out a knife to the boy – Michael McCarthy?
ANSWER	No, sir, but when he was a kid I used put my hand in my pocket to frighten him, for he was a wild young gaffer.
QUESTION	Did you ever try to make an appointment with the eldest girl – Mary McCarthy – Molly's daughter?
ANSWER	No, but if I met her on the road I would say "am I going," and "what time would she be out to-night," and the reply I would get would be "no," a sort of grunt, I never laid a hand on the girl.
QUESTION	Did Molly Carthy ever suggest to you that you were the father of the last child?

ANSWER	No, sir.
QUESTION	Have you heard that she said you were?
ANSWER	No, sir, so far as I know she never named anybody for it.
QUESTION	Did you ever meet or see Molly Carthy out late at night?
ANSWER	No, but I heard she used to be out late herself and some of the boys, and she usually had one of them with her if she was passing this way late to the village.
QUESTION	When was the last time you were talking to Molly McCarthy?
ANSWER	About three weeks or a month ago. I had a few words with her over a goat of hers trespassing on our fields one day about that time. We had a few words in the shed field opposite her door. Michael McCarthy was on his own ditch at the time.
QUESTION	Your uncle has a shot gun; did you ever use it?
ANSWER	I did. I fired one shot at crows out of it last harvest after cutting the wheat. I did not use it since.
QUESTION	When to your knowledge was it used last by any person?
ANSWER	In or about a fortnight ago I heard a shot fired near our house. I was out ploughing in the field at the time. When I returned to the house I asked my uncle what he was firing at and he said he was firing at crows that were taking potatoes out of the small pit in the haggard which was not covered with clay.
QUESTION	Did Tommy Reid ever use your uncle's gun?
ANSWER	Never to my knowledge.
QUESTION	Who cleans your uncle's gun?
ANSWER	The boss. I never cleaned it.
QUESTION	Where was the gun kept?
ANSWER	In the boss's sleeping room.
QUESTION	Where was the gun on Wednesday and Thursday last?
ANSWER	The gun is always kept in the boss's sleeping room.
QUESTION	Do you know when the gun was last cleaned?
ANSWER	I couldn't tell you sir.
QUESTION	Did you know the method by which the gun was cleaned?
ANSWER	No, but I know a yoke was there to clean it. I could not tell you where that yoke was.
QUESTION	Did you discuss the death of Molly Carthy with any person?
ANSWER	No, except Tommy Reid. I said to him "any questions the Guards will ask you tell them the truth, and everything you know."
QUESTION	When did you tell that to Tommy Reid?

ANSWER	After dinner on the day I found the body. That was the first time I mentioned the death to Tommy Reid.
QUESTION	Who fenced the front of the potato pit?
ANSWER	I did.
QUESTION	How did you fence it?
ANSWER	When I was fencing the front of the pit I put bags up against the mouth of the pit next the spuds and then put on the weeds.
QUESTION	What clothes were you wearing last Wednesday and Thursday?
ANSWER	The ones I was wearing to-day except the shirt. I put on the shirt I was wearing to-day yesterday. The shirt I was wearing on last Wednesday and Thursday was the soiled one with the stain on the neck which I gave you to-day.

I have heard this statement read over to me and it is correct.

HARRY GLEESON

Witness:Thomas Reilly, Inspector 26.11.40
Patk. Mahony, Supt. 26.11.40
at 1.10 a.m.

Appendix II

The People v. Henry Gleeson: *Dramatis Personae*

Daly, Anthony.
: (1892-1971). IRA police officer 1918-1922. Joined Garda Siochana 1922; served Cos. Kerry, Meath, Louth, Wicklow, Cavan, Tipperary. Transferred from Ballingarry, Co. Tipperary to New Inn, Co. Tipperary, 1940. Retired 1948.

MacBride, Seán.
: (1904-1988). Fought in War of Independence; present in London during Anglo-Irish Treaty negotiations in 1921; Chief-of-Staff of IRA in 1930s; journalist on *Irish Press,* called to Bar 1937; Senior Counsel, 1943; Minister for External Affairs, 1948-51; Nobel and Lenin awards.

McCarthy, Joseph A.
: (1884-1962). Called to Bar, 1917; Senior Counsel, 1933; Circuit Judge, 1945-1956.

McGrath, Dr. John.
: (1901-1957). Graduate in science and medicine of NUI; consultant to leading Dublin hospitals; Professor of Medical Jurisprudence & Pathology, UCD. State Pathologist 1929-1953.

Maguire, C. Martin.
: (1889-1962). Called to Bar, 1911; Senior Counsel, 1925; High Court judge, 1940-1954; Supreme Court Judge, 1954-1961.

Mahony, Patrick.
: (1897-1980). Joined Garda Siochána 1923; Sergt. 1924; Inspector, 1925; Supt. 1934; retired 1962.

Murnaghan, George.
: (1907-1990). Called to Bar, 1930; Senior Counsel, 1942; High Court judge, 1953-1979.

Nolan-Whelan, James.
: (1893-1950). Called to Bar, 1904; Senior Counsel, 1937.

O'Malley, Fr. James.
: (1871-1953). Ordained priest, Thurles 1899; served in New Zealand, 1988-1911; Templemore, 1911-1919, Galbally, 1919-1932; parish priest of New Inn, 1932-1953.

Timoney, John J.
: (1910-1961). Qualified as solicitor, 1935; Clann na Poblachta TD, 1947-1951.

Troy, Seán.
: (1881-1972). Qualified as solicitor, 1907; for 16 years solicitor to Fermoy UDC; member of Gaelic League, IRB, GAA; judge in Republican Courts, 1919-1922; District Justice, 1922-1951.